AN ENTERTAINMENT DIRECTORY

Where to Shop, Where to Dine,
Attractions and Nightlife

EGP
Editorial

E.G.P. Editorial S.A., 2015

Cuba Travel Guide 2015

© Yardley G. Castro, 2015
© E.G.P. Editorial S.A., 2015

Printed in USA.

ISBN-13: 978-1503313026
ISBN-10: 1503313026

E.G.P. Editorial S.A., 2015

INDEX

WELCOME TO CUBA

Cuba is an island brimming with vibrant art, soul-stirring music and villages cloaked in colonial charm. Home to nine UNESCO World Heritage Sites and a population as warm and scintillating as its tropical climate and colorful arts.

Cuba, the biggest island in the Caribbean, is located at the entrance to the Gulf of México. Cuba's nearest neighbors are: to the East, Haití (77 kilometers), to the West, the Yucatan Peninsula (210 kilometers), to the North, Florida Peninsula (180 kilometers) and to the South, Jamaica (140 kilometers). The Bahamas are very near, toward the Northwest of the eastern end of Cuba. Formed by around 4,195 smaller keys, cays and islets, it covers a surface of 110,922 square kilometers and 1,200 kilometers of extension, on a mostly karstic and flat territory. Its nature, diverse and prodigal, shows wide variety of plants, animals and more than 280 beaches, Virgin Islands, grottos, caves, mountains, forests, savannas and marshes.

The island is divided into 15 provinces and one special municipality, Isla de la Juventud. Notable Cuba areas include rural Pinar Del Río, where tobacco farming builds economic momentum; seaside Santiago de Cuba, the country's second largest city next to Havana rife with colorful Afro-Cuban influence; and colonial Trinidad, a sleepy town designated a UNESCO world heritage site nestled between majestic mountains and the sea.

Cuba's population is richly diverse, with 11.2 million residents. Despite its Native roots, the most profound effects on Cuban culture are the result of European, African and North American influences.

Climate

Moderate subtropical. The Cuban territory grazes the Tropic of Cancer, and due to its long and narrow configuration, on an east-west axis, it receives the refreshing action of the trade winds and the sea breezes. During the short winter, it is cooled by masses of cold air from the North; those cold fronts do not last long. The day and night temperatures differ less in the coastal regions than inland. The eastern part of the country has a warmer climate than the western part.

Temperature

Average temperature 24, 6º C (76, 3º F) Summer average 25º C (77º F) Winter average 22º C (71, 6º F)

Seasons

There are two, clearly defined: the dry season, from November through April; and the rainy season, from May through October. The average annual precipitation is 1 375 mm.

Orography

There are three outstanding large mountain ranges. In the West, the Sierra de los Órganos; in the central part, the Sierra del Escambray; and in the southern region of eastern Cuba, the Sierra Maestra, where the highest point of the country is located, the Pico Real del Turquino, 1 974 meters above the sea level. Its longest river is the Cauto, with a length of 250 kilometers.

History

Cuba was discovered by Christopher Columbus, on October 27, 1492. The conquest and colonization caused the extermination of the aboriginal inhabitants, due to which they imported black people from Africa to enslave them. The resulting mixture defined Cuba's population and culture. On October 10, 1868, the Cuban people began their struggle for independence from Spain, whose colonial rule lasted 4 centuries. United States intervened in the warlike conflict and established a pseudorepublic in 1902 until the 1st. of January of 1959, when the Revolution commanded by Fidel Castro triumphed, bringing essential transformations for the life of the country.

Economy

The tourism is the main line. Other important industries are the sugar cane, tobacco, nickel, rum, coffee, and since a few years ago, the pharmaceutics and biotechnological lines.

Education

Education is free and obligatory until the ninth grade. In 1961, illiteracy was eradicated and today the population has a high instruction level. Cuba's national system of education comprehends from day care centers for working mothers' children to universities disseminated throughout the whole country.

Culture

A country prodigal in artistic and creative manifestations. It has made contributions to international culture with important names of writers, thinkers, dancers, musicians, painters, poets and singers. Cuban craftwork is interesting, with outstanding works in leather, vegetable fibers, wood, stone, metal and sea products. Cuba's cultural infrastructure consists of theaters, museums, art galleries and cinemas, where not only samples of the national wealth of all times are shown, but also of world art. It is the seat of important international events such as the Ballet Festival, the biennial of visual arts, popular music festivals and the Festival of the New Latin American Cinema, among others.

Health

Cuba's health system is said to have one of the world's most complete programs of primary attention, the lowest of infantile mortality rate in Latin America and free services for all the people.

Sports

Excellent Olympic results, a highlighted place in world sports and the massive and free practice in the country make Cuba proud and are counted among the achievements of the people in the past 40 years.

Religion

Lay country with freedom of cults. Catholic and Afro-Cuban religions prevail, although other tendencies also exist.

Payment Forms

In tourist facilities and other service units, prices are set in Cuban Convertible Pesos (CUC). In Varadero, Cayo Largo del Sur, Jardines del Rey (Coco and Guillermo Keys), Santa Lucía and Covarrubias Beaches, and Holguín province (tourist resorts on northern coastline), you can also pay in Euros. Credit cards – except those issued by US banks or their branches in other countries – are accepted. Among those accepted are MasterCard, Visa International and CABAL. Cuban convertible pesos and coins equivalent to 50, 25, 10, 5 and 1 cents have unlimited legal course in the national territory. Cuban convertible pesos can be changed upon departure at bank offices at international airports and ports in Cuba. Traveler's checks, including those issued by US banks, are accepted.

Official Commemorations

Although they are not holidays, they are also considered important dates: January 28: Anniversary of the birth of José Martí, Cuba's National Hero, in 1853. February 24: Anniversary of the beginning of the War of Independence, in 1895. March 8: International Woman's Day. March 13: Anniversary of the attack to the Presidential Palace of Havana, by a group of revolutionary youths that sought to execute the tyrant Fulgencio Batista, in 1957. April 19: Anniversary of the defeat of the mercenary attack at the Bay of Pigs, in 1961. July 30: Day of the Martyrs of the Revolution. October 8: Anniversary of the death of Major Ernesto Ché Guevara, in 1967. October 28: Anniversary of Major Camilo Cienfuegos' death, in 1959. November 27: Commemoration of the execution of eight students of Medicine, by the Spanish colonial government, in 1871. December 7: Anniversary of Antonio Maceo's death in combat in 1896, an outstanding figure in Cuba's War of Independence against the Spanish colonial rule.

Migratory Regulations

Visitors should possess an effective passport or a trip document stating their name and the corresponding visa or Tourist Card, excepting those countries that Cuba maintains Free Visa agreements with. Tourist Cards can be requested at the Cuban consular representations. Also, in travel agencies and airlines. They are of two types: for individual tourists or tourists that travel in groups. The businessmen, journalists at work and natural of Cuba, non-residents or with another nationality, should get a visa.

Sanitary Regulations

There are only restrictive sanitary regulations for visitors coming from countries where yellow fever and endemic cholera exist or have been declared infection areas by the World Health Organization. In such cases, an International Vaccination Certificate is demanded. Products of animal and vegetable origin have entry restrictions. Animals may be imported, previous presentation of the corresponding certificate.

Electricity

The electric appliances endowed with round spikes should be brought with an adapter of plane spikes that are the type used for the plugs existent in the country. Electric current of general use is 110 V / 60 Hz, although in the recently constructed hotels it is 220 V / 60 Hz.

Currency

The national currency is the Cuban Peso, which is equivalent to 100 centavos (cents). Notes can be of 1, 3, 5, 10, 20, 50 and 100 pesos. Coins can be of 1, 5 and 20 centavos, and there are others of 1 and 3 pesos. At the Bureaus of Exchange (CADECA) created to sell - buy Cuban Convertible Pesos, the exchange rate can vary now between $20.00 and $25.00 Cuban pesos to the Cuban Convertible Pesos (CUC). The exchange rate to the American dollar is fixed $ 1.00 CUC - $ 0.87 USD

TRAVEL TIPS

You must be aware of some customs regulations before you travel to Cuba, for example: no weapons, explosives or pornographic magazines are allowed in the country; those tourists arriving from the States, either directly or from a third country, are not permitted to bring videocassette players. Tourist are allowed to bring, tax free, two bottles of liquor, one carton of cigarettes, personal belongings and jewels, photographic and video cameras, typewriters, sports and fishing gear. You can bring, duty free, up to 10 kilos of medicines in their original packaging.

Clothing should be light, mainly during summer, so it would be best to wear shorts, cotton and flannel outfits and sandals. As for winter, a light jacket or a fine wool sweater and closed comfortable shoes would do, mainly at night. You should also bring sunglasses and a bathing-suit and so that you can take a refreshing swim, and don't forget your sunscreen.

The voltage in most residential and trade areas, offices and hotels are 110 V / 60 HZ, though some facilities already have 220 V / 60 HZ. Wall outlets are for flat plugs.

You should not take urban transportation - like the "camel" -; they are always crowded and unreliable. You should take taxis or tourist buses instead, or walk when its short distances. If you want to go on a tour of the island, your best option is to rent a car. There are several car rental offices at the airports, hotels and tourist spots providing high quality cars and services.

You must show your passport and driver's license in order to rent a car. The driver must be at least 21 years old; the license could be international or from your country but at least a year old. It is not advisable to drive at night. You must also watch out for animals on the road and cyclists in urban areas when you are driving. Park the car in a safe well-lit place and do not leave anything valuable in it. You are liable for traffic fines; failure to pay would mean incurring a debt with the State. We recommend you buy a "Road Guide of Cuba" which is very helpful for finding your way around on the roads.

There is no need to be vaccinated to come to Cuba. Most hotels provide 24-hours health care services with specialists and nurses. There are specialized clinics for tourists in the main cities.

Though tap water is drinkable, we advise you to drink bottled water to avoid tropical illnesses.

Even though Cuba is a safe and has a low crime-rate, you should take some precautions to avoid being caught out by petty thieves, who are just waiting for the chance to grab any belonging such as wallets, photo and video cameras, pieces of luggage, handbags or shopping bags. Public peace is ensured in streets by lots of young police officers always willing to help in case you need them, though they do not speak English. You should take note of the following advice: do not take more money with you than you need; do not be careless with your belongings and purchases; take good care of your wallet and passport in crowded places, we suggest you keep them in your front pocket; check the bill at restaurants; get rid of so-called "tourist guides", they are not professional and many are not aware of Cuban history and culture, they just pretend to be nice to tourists in order to fool them; keep your jewels and valuables in the room safe.

Most hotels, restaurants, bars, shops, etc., take Visa and MasterCard credit cards, as long as they are not issued by American banks. However, you should have some cash on you just in case the machines are not working.

Shop, eat, relax and enjoy...

WHERE TO SHOP
(VARADERO)

8 000 Taquillas
Department store
Ave. Playa e/ 53 y 54.
Cárdenas. Matanzas

Josone
Department store
Calle 1ra. e/ 58 y 59.
Cárdenas. Matanzas
Phone: (53 45) 66-7898

Arenas Doradas
Department store
Hotel Arenas Doradas.
Cárdenas. Matanzas
Phone: (53 45) 66-8332

Kawama
Department store
Hotel Kawama. Cárdenas.
Matanzas
Phone: (53 45) 66-7183

Arte 63
Handicrafts
Calle 63 e/ 1ra. y 2da.
Cárdenas. Matanzas
Phone: (53 45) 61-2156

Kawama Sport
Department store
Ave. 1ra. y 63.
Cárdenas. Matanzas
Phone: (53 45) 61-2934

Arte Nuevo
Handicrafts
Calle 63 y 2da.
Cárdenas. Matanzas
Phone: (53 45) 61-2888

Barlovento
Department store
Hotel Iberostar Barlovento.
Cárdenas. Matanzas
Phone: (53 45) 66-7701

Barracuda
Department store
Calle 1ra. y 60.
Cárdenas. Matanzas
Phone: (53 45) 66-3481

La Casa del Habano
Cigar shop
Calle 63 e/ 1ra. y 3ra.
Cárdenas. Matanzas
Phone: (53 45) 66-7186

Brisas
Department store
Hotel Brisas del Caribe.
Cárdenas. Matanzas
Phone: (53 45) 66-7622

Vídeo Centro
Music
Calle 28 y 1ra.
Cárdenas. Matanzas
Phone: (53 45) 66-7706

Tortuga
Department store
Hotel & Villas Tortuga.
Cárdenas. Matanzas
Phone: (53 45) 61-2066

Galería de Arte Varadero
Handicrafts
Calle 1ra. y 39.
Cárdenas. Matanzas
Phone: (53 45) 66-7554

Bazar Hicacos
Handicrafts
Calle 1ra. e/ 33 y 34.
Cárdenas. Matanzas
Phone: (53 45) 61-3663

**La Casa del Tabaco
Club Puntarena**
Cigar shop
Hotel Club Puntarena.
Cárdenas. Matanzas

Bazar Varadero
Handicrafts
Calle 1ra. e/ 44 y 46.
Cárdenas. Matanzas
Phone: (53 45) 61-2329

Las Morlas
Department store
Hotel Las Morlas.
Cárdenas. Matanzas
Phone: (53 45) 61-3913

Bella Costa
Department store
Hotel Bella Costa.
Cárdenas. Matanzas
Phone: (53 45) 66-7596

Los Delfines
Department store
Villa Los Delfines.
Cárdenas. Matanzas
Phone: (53 45) 61-4715

Glamour
Boutique
Ave. Playa y 29.
Cárdenas. Matanzas
Phone: (53 45) 66-7707

WHERE TO SHOP
(VARADERO)

Marina Chapelín
Department store
Carretera Las Morlas.
Cárdenas. Matanzas
Phone: (53 45) 66-7096

Cabañas del Sol
Department store
Carretera Las Américas.
Cárdenas. Matanzas
Phone: (53 45) 61-3466

Meliá Las Américas
Commercial Center
Hotel Meliá Las Américas.
Cárdenas. Matanzas
Phone: (53 45) 66-7600

Caimán
Commercial Center
Calle 1ra. e/ 61 y 62.
Cárdenas. Matanzas
Phone: (53 45) 66-7692

Meliá Las Antillas
Department store
Hotel Meliá Las Antillas.
Cárdenas. Matanzas
Phone: (53 45) 66-8470

Caminos del Mar
Commercial Center
Calle 12 e/ 1ra. y Playa.
Cárdenas. Matanzas
Phone: (53 45) 61-2835

Meliá Varadero
Department store
Hotel Meliá Varadero.
Cárdenas. Matanzas
Phone: (53 45) 66-7013

Kiosko Artex
Music
Calle 1ra. y 47.
Cárdenas. Matanzas
Phone: (53 45) 61-2249

La Abejita
Souvenirs
Calle 1ra. e/ 25 y 26.
Cárdenas. Matanzas
Phone: (53 45) 66-7736

Bazar Cuba
Department store
Calle 64 y 1ra.
Cárdenas. Matanzas
Phone: (53 45) 66-7691

La Casa del Habano
Varadero
Cigar, Rum and Coffee store
Calle 39 y Ave. 1ra.
Cárdenas. Matanzas
Phone: (53 45) 61-4719

Casa de la Miniatura
Handicrafts
Calle 10 y Camino del Mar.
Cárdenas. Matanzas

Grocery Plaza América
Market
Ave. Las Américas km. 11.
Cárdenas. Matanzas
Phone: (53 45) 66-8181

Galería Palma Real
Department store
Ave. 2da. e/ 61 y 62.
Cárdenas. Matanzas
Phone: (53 45) 66-7898

Caracol
Boutique
Plaza Las Américas.
Cárdenas. Matanzas
Phone: (53 45) 66-8551

Mini Super Bello Sol
Market
Calle 63 e/ 1ra. y 3ra.
Cárdenas. Matanzas
Phone: (53 45) 61-2690

Casa de Antigüedades
Handicrafts
Centro Comercial "Plaza
América". Cárdenas. Matanzas

Mini Super Cabañas del Sol
Market
Carretera Las Américas.
Cárdenas. Matanzas
Phone: (53 45) 66-7185

Casa de la Artesanía
Latinoamericana
Handicrafts
Calle 64 y 1ra.
Cárdenas. Matanzas
Phone: (53 45) 66-7691

Mini Super Herradura
Market
Hotel Herradura.
Cárdenas. Matanzas
Phone: (53 45) 66-7697

Tienda Artex
Music
Calle 60 No. 208 esq. a 3ra.
Cárdenas. Matanzas
Phone: (53 45) 66-7415

WHERE TO SHOP
(VARADERO)

Mini Super Pelícano
Market
Villa La Mar.
Cárdenas. Matanzas
Phone: (53 45) 66-7695

Copey
Commercial Center
Calle 3ra. e/ 61 y 63.
Cárdenas. Matanzas
Phone: (53 45) 66-7690

Mini Super Playazul
Market
Calle 13 e/ 1ra. y Playa.
Cárdenas. Matanzas
Phone: (53 45) 61-7867

Coral Negro
Jewelry
Hotel Sol Palmeras.
Cárdenas. Matanzas
Phone: (53 45) 66-7009

Noi
Department store
Calle 1ra. e/ 13 y 14.
Cárdenas. Matanzas
Phone: (53 45) 66-7632

Cuatro Palmas
Department store
Hotel Cuatro Palmas.
Cárdenas. Matanzas
Phone: (53 45) 66-7187

Photoservice Calle 64
Photography
Calle 64 No. 526, Varadero.
Cárdenas. Matanzas
Phone: (53 45) 61-3810

El Encanto
Department store
Calle 1ra. y 42.
Cárdenas. Matanzas
Phone: (53 45) 61-3632

Plaza América
Commercial Center
Carretera Las Américas km. 11
Cárdenas. Matanzas
Phone: (53 45) 66-8181

El Monarca
Department store
Ave. Las Américas km. 11
Cárdenas. Matanzas
Phone: (53 45) 66-7600

Plaza de los Artesanos
Handicrafts
Ave. 1ra. e/ 44 y 46. Cárdenas.

Electrónica Granma
Department store
Calle 31 e/ 1ra. y 3ra.
Cárdenas. Matanzas
Phone: (53 45) 66-7700

Puerta al Sol
Department store
Villas Punta Blanca.
Cárdenas. Matanzas
Phone: (53 45) 61-2362

Feria Caracol
Department store
Calle 1ra. e/ 53 y 57. Cárdenas.

Punta Blanca
Department store
Villas Punta Blanca. Cárdenas.
Phone: (53 45) 61-7871

Fondo Cubano de Bienes Culturales
Handicrafts
Calle 59 esq. a Ave. 1ra.
Cárdenas. Matanzas
Phone: (53 45) 66-7454

Puntarena
Commercial Center
Hotel Club Puntarena.
Cárdenas. Matanzas
Phone: (53 45) 66-7181

Foto Express
Photography
Calle 1ra. e/ 41 y 42.
Cárdenas. Matanzas
Phone: (53 45) 66-7015

Romeo y Julieta
Department store
Calle 63 e/ 1ra. y 3ra.
Cárdenas. Matanzas
Phone: (53 45) 66-7362

Foto Vídeo Varadero
Photography
Calle 1ra. y 42, Edificio Marbella.
Cárdenas. Matanzas

Sol Palmeras
Commercial Center
Hotel Sol Palmeras.
Cárdenas. Matanzas
Phone: (53 45) 66-7009

Galería "Arte, Sol y Mar"
Handicrafts
Ave. 1ra. e/ 34 y 36.
Cárdenas. Matanzas
Phone: (53 45) 61-3153

WHERE TO SHOP
(VARADERO)

Super Club

Department store
Hotel Breezes Varadero.
Cárdenas. Matanzas
Phone: (53 45) 66-7030

**Galería Club Amigo
Varadero**

Commercial Center
Hotel Club Amigo Varadero.
Cárdenas. Matanzas
Phone: (53 45) 66-8243

Taller Cerámica CERVAR

Handicrafts
Calle 60 esq. a Ave. 1ra.
Cárdenas. Matanzas
Phone: (53 45) 66-7829

Tropical

Department store
Hotel Club Tropical.
Cárdenas. Matanzas
Phone: (53 45) 66-7723

Gaviota

Commercial Center
Hotel Sol Sirenas-Coral.
Cárdenas. Matanzas
Phone: (53 45) 66-8070

Tuxpan

Department store
Hotel Tuxpan.
Cárdenas. Matanzas
Phone: (53 45) 66-7560

Internacional

Commercial Center
Hotel Varadero Internacional.
Cárdenas. Matanzas
Phone: (53 45) 66-7693

Villa Cuba

Department store
Villa Cuba Resort.
Cárdenas. Matanzas
Phone: (53 45) 66-7699

WHERE TO SHOP
(HAVANA COLONIAL)

Almacenes Siboney
Department store
Calle Monte esq. a Carmen.
La Habana Vieja. La Habana
Phone: (53 7) 862-1575

La Bella Cubana
Department store
Calle Oficios esq. a Lamparilla.
La Habana Vieja. La Habana
Phone: (53 7) 860-6524

Amadeo
Department store
Calle San Rafael y Monserrate.
La Habana Vieja. La Habana
Phone: (53 7) 863-6885

**La Casa del Café
Mamá Inés**
Cigar, Rum and Coffee store
Calle Baratillo esq. a Obispo.
La Habana Vieja. La Habana
Phone: (53 7) 33-8061

Avenida del Puerto
Market
Calle Oficios e/ Luz y Acosta.
La Habana Vieja. La Habana
Phone: (53 7) 860-6255

La Casa del Habano
Cigar shop
Hotel Conde de Villanueva.
La Habana Vieja. La Habana
Phone: (53 7) 862-9293

Belén
Market
Calle Compostela e/ Jesús María
y Merced. La Habana Vieja.
Phone: (53 7) 860-9475

**La Casa del Habano
Palacio de la Artesanía**
Cigar shop
Calle Cuba No. 64.
La Habana Vieja. La Habana

Benetton
Clothes
Calle Oficios No. 152 esq. a
Amargura. La Habana Vieja.

**La Casa del Tabaco
y del Ron**
Cigar shop
Calle Obispo e/ Bernaza y
Monserrate. La Habana Vieja.
La Habana

Boutique Capitolio
Handicrafts
Paseo del Prado y Teniente Rey,
Capitolio de La Habana.
La Habana Vieja. La Habana

La Distinguida
Department store
Calle Obispo e/ Bernaza y
Villegas. La Habana Vieja.
La Habana

Casa Cofiño
Furniture
Calle Neptuno e/ San Nicolás
y Manrique. Centro Habana.
Phone: (53 7) 33-8086

La Equidad
Department store
Calle Consulado y Neptuno.
La Habana Vieja. La Habana
Phone: (53 7) 863-3829

Casa del Habano
Cigar shop
Calle Mercaderes No. 120 e/
Obispo y Obrapía. La Habana
Vieja. La Habana

La Felicidad
Department store
Calle Monserrate esq. a
Lamparilla. La Habana Vieja.
Phone: (53 7) 860-8166

Casa del Navegante
Nautical Charters
Calle Mercaderes No. 115 e/
Obispo y Obrapía. La Habana
Vieja. La Habana
Phone: (53 7) 861-3625

La Filosofía
Department store
Calle Neptuno esq. a San
Nicolás. Centro Habana.
Phone: (53 7) 33-8603

Casa del Tabaco
Cigar shop
Hostal Valencia.
La Habana Vieja. La Habana
Phone: (53 7) 867-1037

La Francia
Department store
Calle Obispo No. 452 esq. a
Aguacate. La Habana Vieja.
Phone: (53 7) 867-1031

Casa Pérez
Department store
Calle Neptuno e/ San Nicolás y
Manrique. Centro Habana.
Phone: (53 7) 863-2380

La Metropolitana

Department store
Calle Aguacate esq. a Obrapía.
La Habana Vieja. La Habana
Phone: (53 7) 860-0171

Clubman

Department store
Calle Obispo No. 514 e/ Villegas
y Bernaza. La Habana Vieja.

La Taberna del Galeón

Cigar, Rum and Coffee store
Calle Baratillo y Obispo.
La Habana Vieja. La Habana
Phone: (53 7) 33-8476

Complejo "La Isla"

Department store
Calle Galiano No. 307
e/ San Miguel y Neptuno.
Centro Habana. La Habana
Phone: (53 7) 33-8993

Langwith

Animals, Accesories and Food
Calle Obispo No. 410
e/ Aguacate y Compostela.
La Habana Vieja. La Habana

Coral Negro Astral

Jewelry
Calle Neptuno No. 362.
Centro Habana. La Habana
Phone: (53 7) 33-8424

Los Marinos

Market
Calle Egido y Monserrate.
La Habana Vieja. La Habana
Phone: (53 7) 862-1773

Coral Negro Capricornio

Jewelry
Calle Aguila No. 353.
Centro Habana. La Habana
Phone: (53 7) 33-8432

Mercado Neptuno

Market
Calle Neptuno e/ San Nicolás
y Manrique. Centro Habana.
La Habana
Phone: (53 7) 33-8619

Coral Negro Gastón Bared

Jewelry
Calle San Rafael e/ Consulado
e Industria. Centro Habana.
La Habana

Monte y Aguila

Department store
Calle Monte esq. a Aguila.
La Habana Vieja. La Habana
Phone: (53 7) 862-7528

Coral Negro Gemenis

Jewelry
Manzana de Gómez.
La Habana Vieja. La Habana
Phone: (53 7) 33-8381

Moure

Department store
Manzana de Gómez.
La Habana Vieja. La Habana
Phone: (53 7) 33-8323

Coral Negro Gentry

Jewelry
Calle Galiano No. 251.
Centro Habana. La Habana
Phone: (53 7) 33-8424

Novator

Boutique
Calle Obispo esq. a Compostela.
La Habana Vieja. La Habana

Cuatro Caminos

Market
Calle Monte No. 256 e/ Matadero
y Manglar. Centro Habana.
La Habana

Palacio de la Artesanía

Commercial Center
Calle Cuba No. 64.
La Habana Vieja. La Habana
Phone: (53 7) 33-8072

Dominó

Department store
Calle San Rafael e Industria.
Centro Habana. La Habana
Phone: (53 7) 33-8393

Palacio San Miguel

Department store
Hotel San Miguel.
La Habana Vieja. La Habana
Phone: (53 7) 862-7656

El Cadete

Shoe stores
Calle Monte No. 401.
La Habana Vieja. La Habana
Phone: (53 7) 33-8045

Palais Royal

Department store
Calle Obispo y Compostela.
La Habana Vieja. La Habana

WHERE TO SHOP
(HAVANA COLONIAL)

El Clip
Watches and Jewelry Immitations
Calle Obispo No. 501 e/ Villegas
y Bernaza. La Habana Vieja.
La Habana
Phone: (53 7) 861-4741

Park View
Department store
Hotel Park View.
La Habana Vieja. La Habana
Phone: (53 7) 861-3293

El Cristal
Department store
Calle San Rafael y Monserrate.
La Habana Vieja. La Habana
Phone: (53 7) 863-6885

Parque Central
Department store
Hotel Parque Central.
La Habana Vieja. La Habana
Phone: (53 7) 66-0890

El Cristo
Market
Calle Teniente Rey No. 503
e/ Cristo y Bernaza.
La Habana Vieja. La Habana
Phone: (53 7) 861-9070

Peerlees
Department store
Calle Neptuno esq. a Zulueta.
La Habana Vieja. La Habana
Phone: (53 7) 33-8179

El Morro
Market
Calle Cárcel No. 105 e/ Morro
y Prado. La Habana Vieja.

Plaza
Department store
Hotel Plaza. La Habana Vieja.
La Habana
Phone: (53 7) 860-8591

El Palacio del Tabaco
Cigar, Rum and Coffee store
Calle Zulueta No. 106
e/ Refugio y Colón.
La Habana Vieja. La Habana
Phone: (53 7) 33-8389

Prado y Animas
Department store
Paseo del Prado esq. a Animas.
La Habana Vieja. La Habana

El Sol Naciente
Department store
Calle Obispo esq. a Villegas.
La Habana Vieja. La Habana

Puerto Carenas
Handicrafts
Ave. del Puerto, Terminal de
Cruceros. La Habana Vieja.
La Habana

Ferretería Neptuno
Hardware
Calle Neptuno No. 753
e/ Lucena y Marquéz González.
Centro Habana. La Habana
Phone: (53 7) 33-8071

Revert
Boutique
Calle Obispo No. 403 esq. a
Compostela. La Habana Vieja.
La Habana

Florida
Department store
Calle Neptuno e/ San Nicolás y
Manrique. Centro Habana.
La Habana

Saldos
Shoe stores
Calle Obispo No. 504 e/ Bernaza
y Villegas. La Habana Vieja.
La Habana

Fornos Chá
Boutique
Calle Neptuno No. 1 esq. a San
Miguel. La Habana Vieja.
La Habana
Phone: (53 7) 867-1032

Salón Crusellas
Perfumes and Silk
Calle Obispo No. 522 e/ Villegas
y Bernaza. La Habana Vieja.

Fundación Ron Havana Club
Liquor store
Calle San Pedro No. 262 e/ Sol
y Muralla. La Habana Vieja.
Phone: (53 7) 861-1900

Sancy
Jewelry
Calle San Rafael y Amistad.
Centro Habana. La Habana
Phone: (53 7) 33-8322

Galería "1903"
Handicrafts
Hotel Palacio O´Farrill.
La Habana Vieja.
Phone: (53 7) 860-5080

WHERE TO SHOP
(HAVANA COLONIAL)

Taller Arteylla
Calle Galiano No. 202 esq. a
Virtudes. Centro Habana.
La Habana
Phone: (53 7) 66-6658

Galería Los Oficios
Handicrafts
Calle Oficios No. 166
e/ Amargura y Teniente Rey.
La Habana Vieja. La Habana

**Tienda Castillo de la
Real Fuerza**
Cigar, Rum and Coffee store
Ave. del Puerto esq. a O'Reilly.
La Habana Vieja. La Habana
Phone: (53 7) 33-8390

Galería Soyú
Handicrafts
Calle Oficios No. 6 e/ Obispo
y Obrapìa. La Habana Vieja.

**Tienda del Tabaco Hotel
Parque Central**
Cigar, Rum and Coffee store
Hotel Parque Central.
La Habana Vieja. La Habana
Phone: (53 7) 867-0890

Habana
Boutique
Calle Obispo No. 415 esq. a
Aguacate. La Habana Vieja.
La Habana

Tienda Tema
Clothes
Calle Galiano esq. a Virtudes.
Centro Habana. La Habana
Phone: (53 7) 863-5944

Harrys Brothers
Department store
Calle Monserrate e/ O'Reilly
y San Juan de Dios. La Habana
Vieja. La Habana
Phone: (53 7) 862-6882

Topeka
Department store
Calle Obispo No. 413 e/
Aguacate y Compostela.
La Habana Vieja. La Habana

Humada
Electronics and Hardware
Calle Obispo No. 502 esq. a
Villegas. La Habana Vieja.
La Habana

Giselle
Shoe stores
Calle San Rafael y Monserrate.
La Habana Vieja. La Habana
Phone: (53 7) 863-6885

Tienda Tema
Handicrafts
Calle San Rafael No. 101 esq. a
Industria. Centro Habana.
Phone: (53 7) 66-9488

Vídeo Centro Ultra
Music
Reina e/ Angeles y Rayo.
Centro Habana. La Habana

Inglaterra
Department store
Hotel Inglaterra. La Habana
Vieja. La Habana
Phone: (53 7) 33-8415

WHERE TO SHOP
(HAVANA CITY)

17 y 26
Department store
Calle 26 e/ 15 y 17, Vedado.
Plaza de la Revolución.
La Habana

La Inesita
Clothes
Calle Obispo No. 508 e/ Villegas
y Bernaza. La Habana Vieja.

300 Aniversario
Department store
Calle Martí No. 460
e/ Céspedes y Agramonte.
La Habana del Este. La Habana
Phone: (53 7) 97-0879

La Isla de Cuba
Commercial Center
Calle Monte No. 251 esq. a
Factoría. Centro Habana.
La Habana
Phone: (53 7) 66-9469

3ra. y 0
Department store
Calle 3ra. y 0, Miramar. Playa.
Phone: (53 7) 204-2551

La Maison
Boutique
Calle 16 No. 701 e/ 7ma. y 9na.,
Miramar. Playa. La Habana
Phone: (53 7) 204-1543

5ta. y 112
Department store
5ta. Ave. y 112, Miramar.
Playa. La Habana
Phone: (53 7) 204-7444

La Mariposa
Department store
Calle Tulipán y San Juan
Bautista, Nuevo Vedado.
Plaza de la Revolución.
Phone: (53 7) 881-0996

5ta. y 42
Commercial Center
Ave. 5ta. A e/ 40 y 42,
Miramar. Playa. La Habana
Phone: (53 7) 204-4321

La Moderna
Department store
Ave. 243 No. 27205 e/ 174 y 276,
Wajay. Boyeros. La Habana
Phone: (53 7) 55-6739

5ta. y 96
Department store
5ta. Ave. esq. a 96,
Miramar. Playa. La Habana
Phone: (53 7) 204-2075

La Onda
Department store
No. 162 Edif. A-55, Alamar.
La Habana del Este. La Habana
Phone: (53 7) 65-2502

Aché
Department store
Guanabacoa. La Habana
Phone: (53 7) 97-5387

La Palma
Department store
Edif. 34, Villa Panamericana.
La Habana del Este. La Habana
Phone: (53 7) 33-8520

Almacenes Toyo
Department store
Calzada 10 de Octubre esq. a
Calzada de Luyanó. Diez de
Octubre. La Habana
Phone: (53 7) 41-5777

La Palma
Department store
Calle Porvenir y Georgia.
Arroyo Naranjo. La Habana

Almacenes Ultra
Department store
Calle Reina No. 109 e/ Rayos y
Angeles. Centro Habana.
Phone: (53 7) 33-8608

La Perla
Department store
La Lisa. La Habana
Phone: (53 7) 33-0529

Almendares
Department store
Calle 49 s/n esq. 28,
Rpto. Kohly. Playa. La Habana
Phone: (53 7) 208-4747

La Pradera
Department store
Hotel La Pradera.
Playa. La Habana
Phone: (53 7) 33-7471

Amistad
Department store
Calle 26 esq. a Zapata.
Plaza de la Revolución.
La Habana
Phone: (53 7) 830-1028

WHERE TO SHOP
(HAVANA CITY)

La Premier

Department store
Calle 11 esq. a 4, Vedado.
Plaza de la Revolución.
La Habana
Phone: (53 7) 33-3487

Amistad

Market
Calle San Lázaro e/ Infanta y
San Francisco. Centro Habana.
Phone: (53 7) 33-5832

La Primera del Cerro

Department store
Calle Santa Catalina y Duarte.
Cerro. La Habana
Phone: (53 7) 66-6361

Arenas Modas

Department store
Playa Guanabo.
La Habana del Este. La Habana
Phone: (53 7) 96-4293

La Quincallera

Department store
Ave. 51 e/ 118 y 120.
Marianao. La Habana
Phone: (53 7) 267-1612

Aster

Laundrymat
Calle 34 No. 304 e/ 3ra. y 5ta.,
Miramar. Playa. La Habana
Phone: (53 7) 204-1622

La Rima

Department store
Reparto Camilo Cienfuegos.
La Habana del Este. La Habana
Phone: (53 7) 95-3961

Atlántico

Department store
Hotel Atlántico.
La Habana del Este. La Habana
Phone: (53 7) 97-1359

La Ruta

Department store
Calzada de Managua y Mantilla
Arroyo Naranjo. La Habana
Phone: (53 7) 57-8083

Bazar 22

Department store
Calle 22 No. 503 e/ 5ta. y 7ma.,
Miramar. Playa. La Habana
Phone: (53 7) 204-1698

La Silueta

Department store
Calzada 10 de Octubre esq. a
Calzada de Luyanó.
Diez de Octubre. La Habana
Phone: (53 7) 57-7045

Boulevar de Tiendas

Commercial Center
Calle 3ra. e/ 78 y 80,
Miramar. Playa. La Habana

La Sirena

Department store
Ave. 51 e/ 132 y 134.
Marianao. La Habana
Phone: (53 7) 267-9076

Capri

Department store
Hotel Capri. Plaza de la
Revolución. La Habana
Phone: (53 7) 832-0511

La Sorpresa

Department store
Virgen del Camino. San Miguel
del Padrón. La Habana
Phone: (53 7) 91-7568

Casa Bella

Department store
7ma. Ave. esq. a 26,
Miramar. Playa. La Habana
Phone: (53 7) 208-9613

La Sorpresa

Clothes
Calle Obispo No. 520 e/ Villegas
y Bernaza. La Habana Vieja.
La Habana

Casa Blanca

Boutique
Hotel Tryp Habana Libre. Plaza
de la Revolución. La Habana
Phone: (53 7) 33-4011

La Tríada

Cigar, Rum and Coffee store
Complejo Morro-Cabaña.
La Habana del Este. La Habana
Phone: (53 7) 66-9154

Casa de Antigüedades

Handicrafts
Calle 36 No. 4704 esq. a 4,
Reparto Kohly.
Playa. La Habana
Phone: (53 7) 204-2776

La Vigía

Commercial Center
Marina Hemingway.
Playa. La Habana
Phone: (53 7) 204-6750

WHERE TO SHOP
(HAVANA CITY)

Casa del Habano
Cigar shop
5ta. Ave. No. 1407 esq. a 16,
Miramar. Playa. La Habana
Phone: (53 7) 204-1185

La Volanta
Department store
Ave. San Miguel del Padrón.
San Miguel del Padrón.
Phone: (53 7) 91-7989

Casa del Tabaco El Espiral
Cigar, Rum and Coffee store
Calle Paseo e/ 17 y 19, Vedado.
Plaza de la Revolución.
Phone: (53 7) 55-3270

Las Brisas
Department store
Villa Mirador del Mar.
La Habana del Este. La Habana
Phone: (53 7) 97-1354

Casa del Tabaco La Cecilia
Cigar, Rum and Coffee store
5ta. Ave. e/ 110 y 112, Miramar.
Phone: (53 7) 204-8062

Lawton
Department store
Calle 15 No. 475 e/ Concepción
y Dolores. Diez de Octubre.
Phone: (53 7) 98-4176

**Casa del Tabaco La
Escogida**
Cigar, Rum and Coffee store
Hotel Comodoro.
Playa. La Habana
Phone: (53 7) 204-0308

Le Salon
Decorations
Calle 1ra. e/ Paseo y A, Vedado.
Plaza de la Revolución.
Phone: (53 7) 55-3705

Casa Grande
Department store
Calle Martí No. 12 e/ Pepe
Antonio y Div. Guanabacoa.
La Habana del Este. La Habana
Phone: (53 7) 97-6616

Los Pinos
Department store
Villa Los Pinos.
La Habana del Este. La Habana
Phone: (53 7) 97-1267

Casa Sánchez
Department store
Calzada de Bejucal s/n esq. a
Cervantes. Diez de Octubre.
Phone: (53 7) 57-8095

Maisí
Department store
Calle Infanta No. 1116.
Centro Habana. La Habana
Phone: (53 7) 33-5116

Casa Suárez
Department store
Calle San Rafael No. 202.
Centro Habana. La Habana
Phone: (53 7) 863-6269

Mariposa
Department store
Hotel Mariposa.
La Lisa. La Habana
Phone: (53 7) 204-9137

Casa Verano
Boutique
Calle 18 No. 4106 e/ 41 y 43,
Miramar. Playa. La Habana
Phone: (53 7) 204-1982

Mégano
Department store
Hotel Mégano.
La Habana del Este. La Habana
Phone: (53 7) 97-1330

Casablanca
Department store
Ave. 1ra. y 36, Miramar. Playa.
Phone: (53 7) 204-4918

Mekong
Department store
Ave. Santa Catalina e/
La Sola y Mayía Rodríguez.
Diez de Octubre. La Habana
Phone: (53 7) 40-7641

Centro Veterinario Almiquí
Animals, Accesories and Food
Calle 164 No. 506 esq. a 5ta. Ave.
Playa. La Habana
Phone: (53 7) 33-6127

Mercadito H
Market
Calle H No. 155 e/ Calzada y
9na., Vedado. Plaza de la
Revolución. La Habana
Phone: (53 7) 33-4362

Club Le Select
Boutique
5ta. Ave. esq. a 30,
Miramar. Playa. La Habana
Phone: (53 7) 204-4001

23

WHERE TO SHOP
(HAVANA CITY)

Miami
Department store
Calle Neptuno No. 460
e/ Manrique y Campanario.
Centro Habana. La Habana
Phone: (53 7) 862-5178

Colorama
Department store
Ave. 41 e/ 28 y 30. Playa.
Phone: (53 7) 204-4392

Mini Super Caribe
Market
Puente de Boca Ciega,
Playa Santa María del Mar.
La Habana del Este.
Phone: (53 7) 96-3416

Complejo Autopista
Department store
Autopista y 244. La Lisa.
Phone: (53 7) 33-7071

Mini Super Las Terrazas
Market
Ave. Las Terrazas e/ 8 y 10,
Playa Santa María del Mar.
La Habana del Este.
Phone: (53 7) 97-1268

Complejo Brimart
Department store
Calzada de 10 de Octubre
e/ Concepción y San Francisco.
Diez de Octubre. La Habana
Phone: (53 7) 41-3294

Mini Super Santa María
Ave. Las Terrazas e/ 6 y 8,
Playa Santa María del Mar.
Phone: (53 7) 97-1326

Copacabana
Department store
Hotel Copacabana. Playa.
Phone: (53 7) 204-1037

**Mini Super Villa
Panamericana**
Market
Villa Panamericana.
La Habana del Este. La Habana
Phone: (53 7) 95-4241

Coral Negro Albita
Jewelry
Calle Infanta No. 204.
Centro Habana. La Habana
Phone: (53 7) 33-5907

Miramar
Department store
Hotel Miramar.
La Habana del Este. La Habana
Phone: (53 7) 96-2507

Coral Negro Primor
Jewelry
Calle Belascoaín esq. a San
Rafael. Centro Habana.
La Habana
Phone: (53 7) 66-6213

Mónaco
Department store
Calle Juan Delgado y Acosta,
Víbora. Diez de Octubre.
La Habana

Coral Negro Volga
Jewelry
Boulevar Santiago de las Vegas.
Boyeros. La Habana
Phone: (53 7) 33-8402

Nacional
Commercial Center
Hotel Nacional de Cuba.
Plaza de la Revolución. La Habana
Phone: (53 7) 33-5722

Danubio
Department store
Calle 26 esq. a 23, Vedado.
Plaza de la Revolución. La Habana
Phone: (53 7) 33-4565

Náutico
Commercial Center
5ta Ave. e/ 152 y 154, Reparto
Náutico. Playa. La Habana
Phone: (53 7) 33-6252

DITA
Electronics and Hardware
Ave. 84 e/ 7ma. y 9na,
Miramar. Playa. La Habana
Phone: (53 7) 204-5119

Nautilius
Department store
Ave. Las Terrazas e/ 9 y 10,
Playa Santa María del Mar.
Phone: (53 7) 97-1277

DITA
Electronics and Hardware
Calle 1ra. e/ Paseo y A, Vedado.
Plaza de la Revolución.
La Habana
Phone: (53 7) 55-3921

Neptuno-Tritón
Commercial Center
Hotel Neptuno-Tritón.
Playa. La Habana
Phone: (53 7) 204-0098

24

WHERE TO SHOP
(HAVANA CITY)

DITA
Electronics and Hardware
Calle 23 e/ L y M, Vedado. Plaza
de la Revolución. La Habana
Phone: (53 7) 55-3278

Palco
Commercial Center
Calle 188 e/ 5ta. Ave. y 1ra.,
Reparto Flores. Playa.
La Habana
Phone: (53 7) 33-2168

DITA
Electronics and Hardware
Calle Calzada No. 475 e/ E y F,
Plaza de la Revolución.
La Habana
Phone: (53 7) 33-4127

Panorama
Department store
Ave. 42 esq. a 23.
Playa. La Habana
Phone: (53 7) 204-9736

DITA
Electronics and Hardware
Calle 3ra. e/ 78 y 80, Miramar.
Playa. La Habana

Photoservice 23 y O
Photography
Calle 23 y O, Vedado.
Plaza de la Revolución.
Phone: (53 7) 33-5031

El Balcón de la Lisa
Department store
La Lisa. La Habana
Phone: (53 7) 267-1873

Photoservice Articolor
Photography
Calle Goss y Acosta.
Diez de Octubre. La Habana
Phone: (53 7) 41-6557

El Batey
Department store
Marina Hemingway,
Hotel y Villa. Playa. La Habana
Phone: (53 7) 204-6816

Photoservice Capricornio
Photography
Calle Aguila y Neptuno.
Centro Habana. La Habana

El Compás
Department store
Ave. 101 esq. a 18. Cotorro.
La Habana
Phone: (53 7) 66-9015

Photoservice Cerro
Photography
Calzada del Cerro No. 1322.
Cerro. La Habana
Phone: (53 7) 870-4557

El Dandy
Department store
Boulevar Santiago de las Vegas.
Boyeros. La Habana
Phone: (53 7) 33-5775

Photoservice Colorama
Photography
Calzada de Güines No. 805.
San Miguel del Padrón.
La Habana
Phone: (53 7) 91-1975

El Diezmero
Department store
Virgen del Camino. San Miguel
del Padrón. La Habana
Phone: (53 7) 55-8408

Photoservice Comodoro
Photography
Hotel Comodoro.
Playa. La Habana
Phone: (53 7) 204-1969

El Faro
Cigar, Rum and Coffee store
Complejo Morro-Cabaña.
La Habana del Este. La Habana
Phone: (53 7) 66-9766

Photoservice Festival
Photography
Calzada de 10 de Octubre
y Carmen. Diez de Octubre.
La Habana

El Festival
Department store
Ave. 28108 e/ 281 y 283.
Boyeros. La Habana

Photoservice Focsa
Photography
Calle 17 y M, Vedado.
Plaza de la Revolución.
La Habana
Phone: (53 7) 66-2112

El Fierro
Boutique
Villa Panamericana, Edif. 1ra.
La Habana del Este.
La Habana

WHERE TO SHOP
(HAVANA CITY)

Photoservice Gala
Photography
Calle L e/ 23 y 25. Plaza de
la Revolución. La Habana
Phone: (53 7) 832-2205

El Palenque
Department store
Calle Martí y Lama.
Guanabacoa. La Habana
Phone: (53 7) 97-9510

Photoservice Galiano
Photography
Calle Galiano No. 512.
Centro Habana. La Habana
Phone: (53 7) 33-8141

El Progreso
Department store
Alamar. La Habana del Este.
La Habana
Phone: (53 7) 55-9379

Photoservice Gama
Photography
Calle 23 e/ 12 y 14. Plaza de
la Revolución. La Habana
Phone: (53 7) 830-6833

El Puente
Department store
Ave. 51 s/n, Arroyo Arenas.
La Lisa. La Habana
Phone: (53 7) 271-9442

Photoservice Guanabacoa
Photography
Calle Martí No. 215.
Guanabacoa. La Habana
Phone: (53 7) 97-8588

El Roble
Cigar, Rum and Coffee store
Calzada del Cerro No. 1417,
Fábrica de ron Bocoy. Cerro.
Phone: (53 7) 870-5642

Photoservice Guanabo
Photography
Calle 5ta. No. 48009.
La Habana del Este. La Habana

El Sol
Department store
Calle 3ra. No. 340, Zona 1,
Alamar. La Habana del Este.
La Habana
Phone: (53 7) 33-8234

Photoservice La Lisa
Photography
Calle 51 y 180. La Lisa.
La Habana
Phone: (53 7) 267-1629

El Taita
Department store
Aparthotel Las Terrazas.
La Habana del Este. La Habana
Phone: (53 7) 97-1685

Photoservice Marianao
Photography
Calle 124 y 49. Marianao.
La Habana
Phone: (53 7) 260-5040

Flores
Market
Calle 176 e/ 1ra. y 3ra., Reparto
Flores. Playa. La Habana
Phone: (53 7) 33-6512

Photoservice Regla
Photography
Martí s/n e/ Agramonte y
Céspedes. Regla. La Habana
Phone: (53 7) 97-7553

Flores
Department store
Calle 178 No. 109 e/ 1ra. y 5ta.,
Rpto Flores. Playa. La Habana
Phone: (53 7) 33-6490

Photoservice Riviera
Photography
Hotel Habana Riviera. Plaza de
la Revolución. La Habana
Phone: (53 7) 33-3867

Floriarte
Flowers y Ornamental Plants
5ta. Ave. e/ 24 y 26, Miramar.
Playa. La Habana
Phone: (53 7) 204-1952

**Photoservice
Santiago de las Vegas**
Photography
Calle 17 esq. a 11. Boyeros.
Phone: (53 7) 66-6046

Focsa
Department store
Calle 17 esq. a M, Vedado. Plaza
de la Revolución. La Habana
Phone: (53 7) 33-3486

Photoservice Tropicoco
Photography
Hotel Tropicoco.
La Habana del Este. La Habana
Phone: (53 7) 97-1084

WHERE TO SHOP
(HAVANA CITY)

**Fondo Cubano
de Bienes Culturales**
Handicrafts
Ave. 47 No. 4702 esq. a 36,
Reparto Kohly. Playa.
La Habana
Phone: (53 7) 204-8005

**Photoservice Villa
Panamericana**
Photography
Edif. 28, Villa Panamericana.
La Habana del Este. La Habana
Phone: (53 7) 95-2106

Foto Vídeo 17 y Paseo
Photography
Calle 17 y Paseo, Vedado.
Plaza de la Revolución.

Plaza Caracol Tropicoco
Department store
Calle 5ta. e/ 464 y 466, Playa
Guanabo. La Habana del Este.

Foto Vídeo 23 y H
Photography
Calle 23 e/ G y H, Vedado.
Plaza de la Revolución.
Phone: (53 7) 66-2120

Primavera
Department store
Calle Martí y E. Hart, Campo
Florido. La Habana del Este.
La Habana

Foto Vídeo 23 y L
Photography
Calle 23 e/ L y M, Vedado.
Plaza de la Revolución.

Puerto Santo
Cigar, Rum and Coffee store
Hotel Tropicoco.
La Habana del Este. La Habana
Phone: (53 7) 97-1652

Foto Vídeo 3ra. y 70
Photography
Calle 3ra. y 70, Miramar.
Playa. La Habana

Punta Brava
Department store
Calle 251 No. 4419 e/ 44 y 46.
La Lisa. La Habana
Phone: (53 7) 208-9370

Foto Vídeo 5ta. y 40
Photography
Calle 5ta. A e/ 40 y 42,
Miramar. Playa. La Habana
Phone: (53 7) 204-6251

Residencial Tarará
Department store
Calle 23 No. 33714 e/ 6 y 6ta.,
Tarará. La Habana del Este.
Phone: (53 7) 97-1684

Foto Vídeo Galerías Paseo
Photography
Calle 1ra. e/ Paseo y A, Vedado.
Plaza de la Revolución.
La Habana
Phone: (53 7) 55-3170

Riviera
Commercial Center
Hotel Habana Riviera. Plaza
de la Revolución. La Habana
Phone: (53 7) 33-3828

Galápago
Department store
Vía Blanca y Tarará.
La Habana del Este. La Habana
Phone: (53 7) 97-1029

Riviera
Department store
Calle Galiano No. 456.
Centro Habana. La Habana
Phone: (53 7) 33-9601

Galería Chateau Miramar
Department store
Hotel Chateau Miramar. Playa.
Phone: (53 7) 204-1952

Santa Fe
Department store
Calle 1ra. y 298, Santa Fe.
Playa. La Habana
Phone: (53 7) 271-0877

Galería Habana
Handicrafts
Calle Línea e/ E y F, Vedado.
Plaza de la Revolución.
Phone: (53 7) 832-7101

Santa Fe
Department store
Ave. 7ma. y 294, Santa Fe.
Playa. La Habana
Phone: (53 7) 208-7239

Galerías Amazonas
Department store
Calle 12 e/ 23 y 25, Vedado.
Plaza de la Revolución.
La Habana
Phone: (53 7) 66-2437

WHERE TO SHOP
(HAVANA CITY)

Sensación

Shoe stores

Calle Belascoaín No. 204.
Centro Habana. La Habana
Phone: (53 7) 33-5766

Galerías Cohiba

Commercial Center

Calle 3ra. e/ Paseo y 2,
Plaza de la Revolución.
La Habana
Phone: (53 7) 33-3636

Sierra Maestra

Department store

Managua. Boyeros. La Habana
Phone: (53 7) 57-9338

Galerías Comodoro

Commercial Center

Hotel Comodoro.
Playa. La Habana
Phone: (53 7) 204-0308

Sierra Maestra

Commercial Center

Calle 1ra. y 0, Miramar.
Playa. La Habana
Phone: (53 7) 204-1484

Galerías de Paseo

Commercial Center

Calle 1ra. e/ Paseo y A,
Plaza de la Revolución.
La Habana
Phone: (53 7) 55-3921

Supermercado 70

Market

Calle 3ra. e/ 68 y 70,
Miramar. Playa. La Habana
Phone: (53 7) 204-2890

Grocery Comodoro

Market

Hotel Comodoro.
Playa. La Habana
Phone: (53 7) 204-0308

Tángana

Boutique

Línea y Malecón, Plaza de
la Revolución. La Habana
Phone: (53 7) 33-4692

H´Upman

Department store

Calle Infanta esq. a Zapata.
Plaza de la Revolución.
La Habana
Phone: (53 7) 33-5956

Tarará

Department store

Calle 7ma. y 2da.
La Habana del Este. La Habana
Phone: (53 7) 33-5510

Habana Libre

Commercial Center

Hotel Tryp Habana Libre.
Plaza de la Revolución.
Phone: (53 7) 33-4011

Tienda Amelia Peláez

Souvenirs

Hotel Tryp Habana Libre.
Plaza de la Revolución.

Havana Golf Club

Department store

Carretera de Vento km. 8.
Boyeros. La Habana
Phone: (53 7) 45-4578

Tienda Artex

Music

Hotel Habana Riviera. Plaza de
la Revolución. La Habana
Phone: (53 7) 33-4051

Horizontes

Department store

Calle Monte No. 115 e/ Antón
Recio y San Nicolás. Centro
Habana. La Habana
Phone: (53 7) 863-3766

Tienda Artex L y 23

Music

Calle L y 23, Vedado. Plaza de
la Revolución. La Habana
Phone: (53 7) 832-0632

Indochina

Department store

Calle N esq. a 23. Plaza de la
Revolución. La Habana
Phone: (53 7) 33-4363

Tienda Artex Miramar

Music

Calle 18 No. 509, Miramar.
Playa. La Habana
Phone: (53 7) 204-1212

Jicarazo

Cigar, Rum and Coffee store

Calle A y Ave. Central.
La Habana del Este. La Habana
Phone: (53 7) 97-3063

Tienda Casa de la Música

Music

Calle 20 No. 3308 esq. a 35,
Miramar. Playa. La Habana
Phone: (53 7) 204-0447

WHERE TO SHOP
(HAVANA CITY)

Kiosko Cuatro Caminos
Clothes
Calle 105 esq. a 100.
Cotorro. La Habana

Tienda de Tabaco Bacará
Cigar, Rum and Coffee store
Cabaret Tropicana. Marianao.
Phone: (53 7) 267-1365

Kiosko Guaicanamar
Calle Carlos M. Céspedes
esq. a Guaicanamar. Regla.

**Tienda de Tabaco
El Aljibe**
Cigar, Rum and Coffee store
Calle 7ma. esq. a 24, Miramar.
Phone: (53 7) 204-1012

Kioskos Fontanar
Department store
Entrada al Reparto Fontanar.
Boyeros. La Habana
Phone: (53 7) 33-5872

**Tienda de Tabaco
El Corojo**
Cigar, Rum and Coffee store
Hotel Meliá Cohiba. Vedado.
Phone: (53 7) 33-3636

La Arcada
Department store
Calle Martí No. 179.
Guanabacoa. La Habana
Phone: (53 7) 66-9351

**Tienda de Tabaco
La Ferminia**
Cigar, Rum and Coffee store
5ta. Ave. y 186, Reparto Flores.

La Barrena
Department store
Reparto Baluarte, Rancho
Boyeros. Boyeros. La Habana
Phone: (53 7) 45-2286

**Tienda de Tabaco La
Giraldilla**
Cigar, Rum and Coffee store
Calle 222 esq. a 37. La Lisa.
Phone: (53 7) 33-1155

La Caribeña
Department store
Concha y Luyanó. San Miguel
del Padrón. La Habana
Phone: (53 7) 55-7181

Palacio de Convenciones
Department store
Calle 146 e/ 11 y 13,
Cubanacán. Playa. La Habana
Phone: (53 7) 202-5511

**La Casa del Habano
Hotel Nacional**
Hotel Nacional de Cuba. Plaza
de la Revolución. La Habana

Tropicoco
Department store
Hotel Tropicoco.
La Habana del Este. La Habana
Phone: (53 7) 97-1662

**La Casa del Habano
La Vigía**
Cigar, Rum and Coffee store
5ta. Ave. y 248, Marina
Hemingway. Playa.
Phone: (53 7) 204-6772

Tulipán
Department store
Ave. Rancho Boyeros No. 909.
Plaza de la Revolución.
Phone: (53 7) 878-3573

**La Casa del Habano
Partagás**
Cigar, Rum and Coffee store
Calle Industria No. 520
e/ Dragones y Barcelona.
Centro Habana. La Habana
Phone: (53 7) 33-8060

Variedades Bello Caribe
Department store
Hotel Bello Caribe. Playa.
Phone: (53 7) 33-0576

La Casa del Tabaco 23 y P
Cigar shop
Calle 23 esq. a P, Vedado.
Plaza de la Revolución.

Vedado
Department store
Hotel Vedado. Plaza de la
Revolución. La Habana
Phone: (53 7) 33-4072

**La Casa del Tabaco
Hotel Tryp Habana Libre**
Cigar shop
Hotel Tryp Habana Libre.
Plaza de la Revolución.

Viazul
Department store
Ave. 26 y Zoológico, Nuevo
Vedado. Plaza de la Revolución.
Phone: (53 7) 881-1413

WHERE TO SHOP
(HAVANA CITY)

La Casita de Piedra
Children´s Clothes
5ta. Ave. y 248, Santa Fe.
Playa. La Habana
Phone: (53 7) 204-6816

Victoria
Department store
Hotel Victoria. Plaza de la
Revolución. La Habana
Phone: (53 7) 33-3510

La Ceiba
Department store
Abel Santamaría.
Boyeros. La Habana
Phone: (53 7) 55-8796

Vídeo Centro
Music
Calle 23 e/ L y M. Plaza de la
Revolución. La Habana
Phone: (53 7) 66-2334

La Comercial
Department store
Calzada de Vento s/n e/
Acosta y 4ta., Casino Deportivo.
Cerro. La Habana
Phone: (53 7) 40-8007

Vídeo Centro
Music
Calle 3ra. No. 1206 e/ 12 y 14,
Miramar. Playa. La Habana
Phone: (53 7) 204-1782

Vídeo Centro Siboney
Music
Autopista y 244. Playa.
La Habana

Vídeo Centro
Music
5ta. Ave. y 86, Miramar.
Playa. La Habana
Phone: (53 7) 204-2302

La Cuevita
Department store
Rpto. Monterrey. San Miguel
del Padrón. La Habana
Phone: (53 7) 91-4946

Vídeo Centro
Music
Calle Ayestarán y Boyeros.
Cerro. La Habana
Phone: (53 7) 66-6051

La Estrella
Department store
Vía Blanca y Durege.
Diez de Octubre. La Habana

Vídeo Centro Max Music
Music
Ave. 41 e/ 28 y 30. Playa.
La Habana
Phone: (53 7) 204-3376

La Feria Caribeña
Department store
Calle 101 s/n e/ 14 y 16.
Cotorro. La Habana
Phone: (53 7) 57-9581

La Giraldilla
Market
Rpto. La Coronela.
La Lisa. La Habana
Phone: (53 7) 33-6489

Villa Panamericana
Commercial Center
Villa Panamericana.
La Habana del Este. La Habana
Phone: (53 7) 95-3606

La Habanera
Jewelry
Calle 12 No. 505 e/ 5ta. y 7ma.
Playa. La Habana
Phone: (53 7) 204-2546

Yumurí
Department store
Calle Belascoaín No. 601.
Centro Habana. La Habana
Phone: (53 7) 33-8606

La Iluminación
Department store
Calzada del Cerro y Arzobispo.
Cerro. La Habana
Phone: (53 7) 40-9109

La Cordial
Department store
Santiago de las Vegas.
Boyeros. La Habana
Phone: (53 7) 57-9317

WHERE TO SHOP
(SANTIAGO DE CUBA)

Albión
Handicrafts
Calle Enramada e/ Calvario y
Carnicería. Santiago de Cuba

La Catedral
Department store
Calle Heredia e/ Félix Pena
y Lacret. Santiago de Cuba
Phone: (53 226) 65-1055

Amistad
Department store
Carretera Central y Donato
Mármol (Edificio 27 de
Diciembre). Palma Soriano.
Santiago de Cuba
Phone: (53 225) 2402

La Escuadra
Hardware
Calle Félix Pena esq. a San
Fernando. Santiago de Cuba
Phone: (53 226) 65-1395

Artesanía
Department store
Hotel Meliá Santiago de Cuba.
Santiago de Cuba
Phone: (53 226) 64-2612

La Granada
Shoe stores
Calle Enramada No. 302.
Santiago de Cuba
Phone: (53 226) 65-1055

Balcón del Caribe
Department store
Hotel Balcón del Caribe.
Santiago de Cuba
Phone: (53 226) 69-1011

La Importadora
Department store
Palma Soriano.
Santiago de Cuba
Phone: (53 225) 2402

Barra del Ron Caney
Cigar, Rum and Coffee store
Calle Peralejo No. 703,
Fábrica de Ron Caney.
Phone: (53 226) 62-5576

La Maison
Boutique
Ave. Manduley No. 52 esq. a
1ra., Reparto Vista Alegre.
Santiago de Cuba
Phone: (53 22) 64-1117

Bucanero
Department store
Hotel Bucanero.
Santiago de Cuba

Las Américas
Department store
Hotel Las Américas.
Santiago de Cuba.

Casa de la Artesanía
Department store
Calle Lacret No. 724
e/ San Basilio y Heredia.
Santiago de Cuba
Phone: (53 226) 62-4027

Las Brisas
Department store
Carretera Central km. 2½,
Alturas de Quintero.
Santiago de Cuba.
Phone: (53 226) 63-2578

Photoservice 4ta. y Garzón
Photography
Calle 4ta. esq. a Garzón.
Santiago de Cuba

El Oasis
Department store
Carretera de Baconao km. 5.
Santiago de Cuba
Phone: (53 226) 63-9227

Photoservice Catedral
Photography
Calle San Pedro e/ San Basilio
y Heredia. Santiago de Cuba
Phone: (53 226) 62-2226

Ensueño
Boutique
Calle Aguilera esq. a Reloj.
Santiago de Cuba
Phone: (53 226) 62-4561

Plaza de Marte
Commercial Center
Calle Garzón No. 4.
Santiago de Cuba
Phone: (53 226) 62-3442

**Fondo Cubano de Bienes
Culturales**
Handicrafts
Calle Lacret No. 704 esq. a
Heredia. Santiago de Cuba
Phone: (53 22) 652358

Primor
Department store
Calle Enramada No. 302.
Santiago de Cuba
Phone: (53 226) 65-1055

WHERE TO SHOP
(SANTIAGO DE CUBA)

Foto Express
Photography
Calle San Pedro e/ José A. Saco
y Carmen. Santiago de Cuba

San Juan
Department store
Hotel San Juan.
Santiago de Cuba
Phone: (53 226) 64-2478

Galería de Arte Universal
Handicrafts
Calle C e/ M y Terrazas,
Reparto Vista Alegre.

Santiago
Boutique
Hotel Meliá Santiago de Cuba.
Santiago de Cuba
Phone: (53 226) 64-2612

Galería Hermanos Tejeda
Handicrafts
Hotel Meliá Santiago de Cuba.
Santiago de Cuba

Tienda Artex
Handicrafts
Calle Heredia No. 304
e/ Carnicería y Calvario.
Santiago de Cuba

Galería La Confronta
Handicrafts
Calle Heredia e/ Carnicería
y San Félix. Santiago de Cuba

Tienda Artex La Catedral
Music
Calle Heredia s/n e/ San Pedro
y Félix Pena. Santiago de Cuba

Galería Oriente
Calle Lacret No. 653 e/ Heredia
y Aguilera. Santiago de Cuba

Tienda Artex La Punta
Music
Carretera de Baconao.
Santiago de Cuba

Galería Santiago
Handicrafts
Calle San Pedro esq. a Heredia.
Santiago de Cuba

Tienda Artex Valle de la Prehistoria
Music
Carretera de Baconao.
Santiago de Cuba

Gaviota
Department store
Villa Santiago de Cuba.
Santiago de Cuba
Phone: (53 226) 68-7166

Trayler El Morro
Department store
Castillo del Morro.
Santiago de Cuba
Phone: (53 226) 69-1527

Ilusión
Department store
Calle 9 esq. a 6. Contramaestre.
Phone: (53 226) 68-9282

Trayler Ferreiro
Department store
Calle 6 No. 409 esq. a 17.
Santiago de Cuba
Phone: (53 226) 64-1901

Internacional
Department store
Hotel Meliá Santiago de Cuba.
Phone: (53 226) 64-2628

Trayler Reloj
Department store
Calle 6 No. 409 esq. a 17.
Santiago de Cuba
Phone: (53 226) 64-1901

La Alameda
Commercial Center
Ave. Lorraine e/ Heredia
y Aguilera. Santiago de Cuba
Phone: (53 226) 65-2078

Versalles
Department store
Hotel Versalles.
Santiago de Cuba
Phone: (53 226) 69-1016

La Casa del Habano Santiago de Cuba
Cigar, Rum and Coffee store
Ave. Jesús Menéndez No. 703.
Santiago de Cuba
Phone: (53 226) 62-2366

Villa Trópico
Department store
Reparto 30 de Noviembre.
Santiago de Cuba
Phone: (53 264) 4-2336

Vista Alegre
Market
Carretera del Caney e/ 13 y 15,
Reparto Vista Alegre.
Santiago de Cuba
Phone: (53 226) 64-1165

WHERE TO SHOP
(HOLGUÍN)

Baybrama
Department store
Hotel Atlántico-Guardalavaca.
Banes. Holguín
Phone: (53 24) 3-0207

La Casa del Tabaco
Guardalavaca
Cigar shop
Playa Guardalavaca.
Banes. Holguín

El Paraíso
Department store
Hotel Brisas Guardalavaca.
Banes. Holguín
Phone: (53 24) 3-0391

La Golondrina
Department store
Hotel Brisas Guardalavaca.
Banes. Holguín
Phone: (53 24) 3-0206

**La Casa del Habano
El Cuje**
Department store
Bungalows Hotel Atlántico-
Guardalavaca. Banes. Holguín
Phone: (53 24) 3-0431

Las Arenas
Department store
Bungalows Hotel Atlántico-
Guardalavaca. Banes. Holguín
Phone: (53 24) 3-0207

Framboyán
Department store
Playa Guardalavaca.
Banes. Holguín

**Photoservice
Guardalavaca**
Photography
Boulevard Hotel Atlántico-
Guardalavaca. Banes. Holguín
Phone: (53 24) 30382

La Aromática
Department store
Hotel Brisas Guardalavaca.
Banes. Holguín
Phone: (53 24) 3-0391

Trayler No. 1
Department store
La Rotonda, Playa
Guardalavaca. Banes. Holguín

Especialidades
Boutique
Hotel Atlántico-Guardalavaca.
Banes. Holguín
Phone: (53 24) 3-0309

La Orquídea
Department store
Hotel Atlántico-Guardalavaca.
Banes. Holguín
Phone: (53 24) 3-0190

Facilidades
Department store
Calle 10 e/ 1ra. y 3ra. Rafael
Freyre. Holguín

Venus
Department store
Hotel Brisas Guardalavaca.
Banes. Holguín
Phone: (53 24) 3-0188

WHERE TO SHOP
(CAYO LARGO DEL SUR)

Aeropuerto Cayo Largo
Department store
Cayo Largo del Sur.
Isla de la Juventud
Phone: (53 45) 248125

**La Casa del Tabaco Hotel
Sol Pelícano**
Cigar shop
Hotel Sol Pelícano.
Isla de la Juventud

Bucanero
Department store
Playa del Pirata, Cayo Largo
del Sur. Isla de la Juventud
Phone: (53 45) 248131

Lindamar
Department store
Villa Lindamar, Cayo Largo
del Sur. Isla de la Juventud
Phone: (53 45) 248023

Capricho
Department store
Villa Capricho, Cayo Largo
del Sur. Isla de la Juventud
Phone: (53 45) 248122

Pelícano
Department store
Hotel Sol Pelícano.
Isla de la Juventud
Phone: (53 45) 248124

Iguana
Department store
Villa Iguana, Cayo Largo
del Sur. Isla de la Juventud
Phone: (53 45) 248121

Photoservice Cayo Largo
Photography
Cayo Largo del Sur.
Isla de la Juventud
Phone: (53 45) 248209

Isla del Sur
Department store
Hotel Isla del Sur, Cayo Largo
del Sur. Isla de la Juventud
Phone: (53 45) 248123

WHERE TO SHOP
(SOROA & VIÑALES)

Soroa
Department store
Villa Soroa.
Candelaria. Artemisa
Phone: (53 85) 2122

El Mogote
Department store
Calle Salvador Cisneros
No. 57 e/ Ceferino Fernández
y J. Pérez. Viñales. Pinar del Río

Los Jazmines
Department store
Hotel Los Jazmines.
Viñales. Pinar del Río
Phone: (53 8) 9-3265

La Ermita
Department store
Hotel La Ermita.
Viñales. Pinar del Río
Phone: (53 8) 9-3204

WHERE TO SHOP
(TRINIDAD)

Aeropuerto Trinidad
Department store
Carretera de Casilda.
Trinidad. Sancti Spiritus
Phone: (53 419) 2547

La Canchánchara
Department store
Calle Rubén Martínez Villena
No. 74. Trinidad. Sancti Spiritus

Ancón
Department store
Hotel Ancón. Trinidad.
Sancti Spiritus
Phone: (53 419) 6120

Casa del Tabaco Trinidad
Cigar shop
Calle Francisco J. Zerquera No.
304 esq. a Maceo.
Trinidad. Sancti Spiritus

Casa del Tabaco Trinidad
Cigar, Rum and Coffee store
Calle José Martí No. 296 esq. a
Parque Trinidad.
Trinidad. Sancti Spiritus
Phone: (53 419) 6149

Las Cuevas
Department store
Hotel Las Cuevas.
Trinidad. Sancti Spiritus
Phone: (53 419) 4013

Casilda
Department store
Calle Real, Casilda.
Trinidad. Sancti Spiritus

Manacas-Iznaga
Department store
Carretera de Sancti Spíritus km.
12, Valle de los Ingenios.
Trinidad. Sancti Spiritus
Phone: (53 419) 7241

Cochera Brunet
Department store
Calle Simón Bolívar No. 501.
Trinidad. Sancti Spiritus
Phone: (53 419) 2139

Mesón del Regidor
Department store
Calle Simón Bolívar No. 312.
Trinidad. Sancti Spiritus

Costasur
Department store
Hotel Costasur. Trinidad.
Sancti Spiritus
Phone: (53 419) 6174

Mini Super La Delicia
Market
Calle Francisco J. Zerquera
No. 7. Trinidad. Sancti Spiritus

El Campesino
Department store
Carretera a Cienfuegos
km. 1½, Finca El Campesino.
Trinidad. Sancti Spiritus
Phone: (53 419) 3581

Photoservice Trinidad
Photography
Hotel Ancón. Trinidad.
Sancti Spiritus

Fondo Cubano de Bienes
Culturales
Handicrafts
Calle Simón Bolívar e/ Ernesto
Valdés y Francisco Gómez Toro.
Trinidad. Sancti Spiritus

Santa Ana
Department store
Calle Camilo Cienfuegos s/n
y J. M. García. Trinidad.
Sancti Spiritus
Phone: (53 419) 3523

Galería de Arte
Handicrafts
Calle Simón Bolívar esq. a Ruben
Martínez Villena. Trinidad.
Sancti Spiritus

Tienda Artex Playa Ancón
Music
Hotel Ancón. Trinidad.
Sancti Spiritus
Phone: (53 419) 6120

Galerías Trinidad
Commercial Center
Calle José Martí s/n e/ Rosario
y Colón. Trinidad. Sancti Spiritus
Phone: (53 419) 2581

Trinidad
Department store
Calle Antonio Maceo No. 442.
Trinidad. Sancti Spiritus

WHERE TO DINE
(VARADERO)

Albacora

Fish and seafood
Calle 59 y Mar.
Cárdenas. Matanzas
Phone: (53 45) 61-3650

La Habana

Buffet restaurant
Hotel Meliá Varadero.
Cárdenas. Matanzas
Phone: (53 45) 66-7013

Antigüedades

Fish and seafood
Calle 1ra. e/ 56 y 58, Parque
Josone. Cárdenas. Matanzas
Phone: (53 45) 66-7329

La Hacienda

Mexican cuisine
Hotel Bella Costa.
Cárdenas. Matanzas
Phone: (53 45) 66-7210

Antillano

Buffet restaurant
Hotel Varadero Internacional.
Cárdenas. Matanzas
Phone: (53 45) 66-7038

La Hacienda

Buffet restaurant
Hotel Iberostar Barlovento.
Cárdenas. Matanzas
Phone: (53 45) 66-7140

Ara

Buffet restaurant
Hotel Paradisus Varadero.
Cárdenas. Matanzas
Phone: (53 45) 66-8700

La Isabelica

Buffet restaurant
Hotel Iberostar Taínos.
Cárdenas. Matanzas
Phone: (53 45) 66-8656

Atenas de Cuba

Cuban cuisine
Hotel Club Amigo Varadero.
Cárdenas. Matanzas
Phone: (53 45) 66-8243

La Isleta

International cuisine
Marina Dársena de Varadero.
Cárdenas. Matanzas
Phone: (53 45) 61-3730

Atlántico

International cuisine
Aparthotel Mar del Sur.
Cárdenas. Matanzas
Phone: (53 45) 61-2246

La Laguna

Cuban cuisine
Hotel Tryp Península
Varadero. Cárdenas. Matanzas
Phone: (53 45) 66-8800

Bacunayagua

Cuban cuisine
Hotel Barceló Marina Palace.
Cárdenas. Matanzas
Phone: (53 45) 66-9966

La Marina

Buffet restaurant
Hotel Barceló Marina Palace.
Cárdenas. Matanzas
Phone: (53 45) 66-9966

Barbecue

Grill
Hotel Playa Alameda
Varadero. Cárdenas. Matanzas
Phone: (53 45) 66-8822

La Panchita

Buffet restaurant
Hotel Sol Palmeras.
Cárdenas. Matanzas
Phone: (53 45) 66-7009

Beach Club
"Ranchón Bucanero"

Light Meals
Hotel Playa Alameda
Varadero. Cárdenas. Matanzas
Phone: (53 45) 66-8822

La Piazza

Italian cuisine
Hotel Palma Real.
Cárdenas. Matanzas
Phone: (53 45) 61-4555

Bello Mar

Light Meals
Hotel Arenas Blancas.
Cárdenas. Matanzas
Phone: (53 45) 61-4450

La Polymita

International cuisine
Hotel & Villas Tortuga.
Cárdenas. Matanzas
Phone: (53 45) 61-4747

Biergarten Prost

Cuban cuisine
Hotel Sol Sirenas-Coral.
Cárdenas. Matanzas
Phone: (53 45) 66-8070

WHERE TO DINE
(VARADERO)

La Robleza
Cuban cuisine
Hotel Meliá Las Américas.
Cárdenas. Matanzas
Phone: (53 45) 66-7600

Bodegón Criollo
Cuban cuisine
Ave. Playa y 40.
Cárdenas. Matanzas
Phone: (53 45) 66-7784

La Sangría
International cuisine
Calle 1ra. e/ 8 y 9.
Cárdenas. Matanzas

Buffet
Buffet restaurant
Hotel Tuxpan.
Cárdenas. Matanzas
Phone: (53 45) 66-7560

La Sirena
Buffet restaurant
Hotel Los Delfines.
Cárdenas. Matanzas
Phone: (53 45) 66-7720

Burgui Varadero
Light Meals
Ave. 1ra. y 43.
Cárdenas. Matanzas
Phone: (53 45) 66-7578

La Taberna
Cuban cuisine
Camino del Mar e/ 13 y 14.
Cárdenas. Matanzas
Phone: (53 45) 61-2223

Café Carnaval
Italian cuisine
Hotel Meliá Las Antillas.
Cárdenas. Matanzas
Phone: (53 45) 66-8470

La Tasca
Buffet restaurant
Hotel Kawama.
Cárdenas. Matanzas
Phone: (53 45) 61-4416

Caguairan
Grill
Hotel Playa Caleta.
Cárdenas. Matanzas
Phone: (53 45) 66-7120

La Terraza
Buffet restaurant
Hotel Meliá Las Américas.
Cárdenas. Matanzas
Phone: (53 45) 66-7600

Capri
Italian cuisine
Calle 42 e/ Ave. y Playa.
Cárdenas. Matanzas
Phone: (53 45) 61-2117

La Terraza
Light Meals
Autopista Sur km. 11, Plaza
América. Cárdenas. Matanzas
Phone: (53 45) 66-8181

Casa de Al
Spanish cuisine
Villa Punta Blanca.
Cárdenas. Matanzas
Phone: (53 45) 66-8050

La Trovatta
Italian cuisine
Hotel Varadero Internacional.
Cárdenas. Matanzas
Phone: (53 45) 66-7038

Casablanca
International cuisine
Hotel Playa Caleta.
Cárdenas. Matanzas
Phone: (53 45) 66-7120

La Vicaria
Cuban cuisine
Ave. 1ra. y 38.
Cárdenas. Matanzas
Phone: (53 45) 61-4721

Castell Nuovo
Italian cuisine
Calle 1ra. y 11.
Cárdenas. Matanzas
Phone: (53 45) 66-7786

La Zarzuela
Spanish cuisine
Hotel Barceló Marina Palace.
Cárdenas. Matanzas
Phone: (53 45) 66-9966

Cayo Libertad
International cuisine
Marina Dársena de Varadero.
Cárdenas. Matanzas
Phone: (53 45) 61-3730

Laguna Azul
Light Meals
Hotel Playa Alameda
Varadero. Cárdenas. Matanzas
Phone: (53 45) 66-8822

WHERE TO DINE
(VARADERO)

Chez Plaza

International cuisine

Autopista Sur km. 11, Plaza
América. Cárdenas. Matanzas

Phone: (53 45) 66-8181

Lai Lai

Asian cuisine

Calle 1ra. y 18.
Cárdenas. Matanzas

Phone: (53 45) 61-3297

Chiringuito

Grill

Hotel Paradisus Varadero.
Cárdenas. Matanzas

Phone: (53 45) 66-8700

Las Américas

International cuisine

Carretera Las Américas
km. 8 ½, Mansión Xanadu.
Cárdenas. Matanzas

Phone: (53 45) 66-7388

Continental

International cuisine

Hotel Varadero Internacional.
Cárdenas. Matanzas

Phone: (53 45) 66-7038

Las Brasas

International cuisine

Camino del Mar y 12.
Cárdenas. Matanzas

Phone: (53 45) 61-2407

Continental

Buffet restaurant

Aparthotel Mar del Sur.
Cárdenas. Matanzas

Phone: (53 45) 61-2246

Las Brisas

International cuisine

Hotel Brisas del Caribe.
Cárdenas. Matanzas

Phone: (53 45) 66-8030

Coral

Buffet restaurant

Hotel Las Morlas.
Cárdenas. Matanzas

Phone: (53 45) 66-7230

Las Dalias

Buffet restaurant

Villa Cuba Resort.
Cárdenas. Matanzas

Phone: (53 45) 66-8280

Coral Negro

Fish and seafood

Calle 1ra. y Punta Blanca.
Cárdenas. Matanzas

Las Olas

Grill

Hotel Las Morlas.
Cárdenas. Matanzas

Phone: (53 45) 66-7230

Crucero

Buffet restaurant

Aparthotel Mar del Sur.
Cárdenas. Matanzas

Phone: (53 45) 61-2246

Las Palmas

Buffet restaurant

Hotel Cuatro Palmas.
Cárdenas. Matanzas

Phone: (53 45) 66-7040

Dante

Italian cuisine

Calle 1ra. e/ 56 y 58, Parque
Josone. Cárdenas. Matanzas

Phone: (53 45) 66-7738

Las Perlas

International cuisine

Hotel & Villas Tortuga.
Cárdenas. Matanzas

Phone: (53 45) 61-4747

Dolce Vita

Italian cuisine

Hotel Arenas Doradas.
Cárdenas. Matanzas

Phone: (53 45) 66-8150

Lindamar

Buffet restaurant

Hotel Barceló Solymar Beach
Resort. Cárdenas. Matanzas

Phone: (53 45) 61-4499

Don Alfredo

Italian cuisine

Hotel Bella Costa.
Cárdenas. Matanzas

Phone: (53 45) 66-7210

Los Bohíos

Grill

Hotel Breezes Varadero.
Cárdenas. Matanzas

Phone: (53 45) 66-7030

Don Alfredo

Italian cuisine

Hotel Playa Alameda Varadero.
Cárdenas. Matanzas

Phone: (53 45) 66-8822

WHERE TO DINE
(VARADERO)

Los Corales
Italian cuisine
Hotel Barceló Solymar Beach
Resort. Cárdenas. Matanzas
Phone: (53 45) 61-4499

Doñaneli
Baking-Pastry
Calle 1ra. y 43.
Cárdenas. Matanzas
Phone: (53 45) 66-7578

Los Corales
Italian cuisine
Hotel Los Delfines.
Cárdenas. Matanzas
Phone: (53 45) 66-7720

El Arlequino
Italian cuisine
Hotel Barceló Marina Palace.
Cárdenas. Matanzas
Phone: (53 45) 66-9966

Los Jardines
Buffet restaurant
Hotel Arenas Blancas.
Cárdenas. Matanzas
Phone: (53 45) 61-4450

El Arrecife
Fish and seafood
Calle 13 y Camino del Mar.
Cárdenas. Matanzas
Phone: (53 45) 61-3787

Mallorca
International cuisine
Calle 1ra. e/ 61 y 62.
Cárdenas. Matanzas
Phone: (53 45) 66-7746

El Brocal
Buffet restaurant
Villas Punta Blanca.
Cárdenas. Matanzas
Phone: (53 45) 66-8050

Marina Chapelín
Fish and seafood
Carretera Las Morlas
km. 12 ½ Cárdenas. Matanzas
Phone: (53 45) 66-7550

El Buho
Buffet restaurant
Hotel Acuazul.
Cárdenas. Matanzas
Phone: (53 45) 66-7132

Martino´s
Italian cuisine
Hotel Breezes Varadero.
Cárdenas. Matanzas
Phone: (53 45) 66-7030

El Cactus
Mexican cuisine
Hotel Iberostar Barlovento.
Cárdenas. Matanzas
Phone: (53 45) 66-7140

Mediterráneo
International cuisine
Calle 54 y 1ra.
Cárdenas. Matanzas
Phone: (53 45) 61-2460

El Candil
Cuban cuisine
Hotel Kawama.
Cárdenas. Matanzas
Phone: (53 45) 61-4416

Mesón del Quijote
International cuisine
Carretera de Las Américas
km. 1, Cárdenas. Matanzas
Phone: (53 45) 66-7796

El Caribeño
Grill
Hotel Sol Palmeras.
Cárdenas. Matanzas
Phone: (53 45) 66-7009

Mi Casita
International cuisine
Camino del Mar e/ 11 y 12.
Cárdenas. Matanzas
Phone: (53 45) 61-3787

El Colibrí
International cuisine
Hotel Tuxpan.
Cárdenas. Matanzas
Phone: (53 45) 66-7560

Mirador
International cuisine
Hotel Bella Costa.
Cárdenas. Matanzas
Phone: (53 45) 66-7210

El Criollo
Cuban cuisine
Villa Cuba Resort.
Cárdenas. Matanzas
Phone: (53 45) 66-8280

Mistral
Buffet restaurant
Hotel Sol Sirenas-Coral.
Cárdenas. Matanzas
Phone: (53 45) 66-8070

WHERE TO DINE
(VARADERO)

El Criollo
Cuban cuisine
Calle 1ra. y 18.
Cárdenas. Matanzas
Phone: (53 45) 61-4794

Oshin
Asian cuisine
Hotel Sol Palmeras.
Cárdenas. Matanzas
Phone: (53 45) 66-7009

El Framboyán
Light Meals
Hotel Barlovento.
Cárdenas. Matanzas
Phone: (53 45) 66-7140

Natura
International cuisine
Hotel Arenas Doradas.
Cárdenas. Matanzas
Phone: (53 45) 66-8150

El Escarpe
Buffet restaurant
Hotel Arenas Doradas.
Cárdenas. Matanzas
Phone: (53 45) 66-8150

Pizza Nova
Italian cuisine
Autopista Sur km. 11, Plaza
América. Cárdenas. Matanzas
Phone: (53 45) 66-8181

El Dorado
Buffet restaurant
Hotel Playa de Oro.
Cárdenas. Matanzas
Phone: (53 45) 66-8566

Palma Real
Buffet restaurant
Hotel Tryp Península Varadero.
Cárdenas. Matanzas
Phone: (53 45) 66-8800

El Fuerte
Buffet restaurant
Hotel Club Tropical.
Cárdenas. Matanzas
Phone: (53 45) 61-3915

Nautilus
Buffet restaurant
Hotel Sun Beach.
Cárdenas. Matanzas
Phone: (53 45) 66-7490

El Faro
Fish and seafood
Hotel Barceló Marina Palace.
Cárdenas. Matanzas
Phone: (53 45) 66-9966

Pizzería
Italian cuisine
Oasis Tennis Centre.
Cárdenas. Matanzas
Phone: (53 45) 66-7380

El Dorado
Buffet restaurant
Villa La Mar.
Cárdenas. Matanzas
Phone: (53 45) 61-3910

Panorama
Light Meals
Hotel Varadero Internacional.
Cárdenas. Matanzas
Phone: (53 45) 66-7038

El Galeón
Buffet restaurant
Aparthotel Mar del Sur.
Cárdenas. Matanzas
Phone: (53 45) 61-2246

O Sole Mio
Italian cuisine
Hotel Sol Palmeras.
Cárdenas. Matanzas
Phone: (53 45) 66-7009

El Flamboyan
International cuisine
Hotel Palma Real.
Cárdenas. Matanzas
Phone: (53 45) 61-4555

Playa Caleta
Cuban cuisine
Hotel Playa de Oro.
Cárdenas. Matanzas
Phone: (53 45) 66-8566

El Dujo
International cuisine
Hotel Sun Beach.
Cárdenas. Matanzas
Phone: (53 45) 66-7490

Papa Fundo
Light Meals
Hotel Acuazul.
Cárdenas. Matanzas
Phone: (53 45) 66-7132

El Galeón
Grill
Hotel Arenas Doradas.
Cárdenas. Matanzas
Phone: (53 45) 66-8150

WHERE TO DINE
(VARADERO)

Puesta de Sol
Cuban cuisine
Villas Punta Blanca.
Cárdenas. Matanzas
Phone: (53 45) 66-8050

El Galeón
Fish and seafood
Marina Gaviota Varadero.
Cárdenas. Matanzas
Phone: (53 45) 61-6296

Pullman
International cuisine
Hotel Pullman.
Cárdenas. Matanzas
Phone: (53 45) 66-7161

El Habanero
Buffet restaurant
Hotel Varadero 1920.
Cárdenas. Matanzas
Phone: (53 45) 66-8288

Quianmen
Asian cuisine
Hotel Sol Sirenas-Coral.
Cárdenas. Matanzas
Phone: (53 45) 66-8070

El Istmo
International cuisine
Hotel Dos Mares.
Cárdenas. Matanzas
Phone: (53 45) 61-2702

Rancho "El Caney"
International cuisine
Calle 1ra. y 40.
Cárdenas. Matanzas

El Marino
Fish and seafood
Hotel Arenas Blancas.
Cárdenas. Matanzas
Phone: (53 45) 61-4450

Ranchón Arizona
International cuisine
Hotel Meliá Las Antillas.
Cárdenas. Matanzas
Phone: (53 45) 66-8470

El Melaíto
Cuban cuisine
Calle 38 y 1ra. Ave.
Cárdenas. Matanzas

Ranchón del Caribe
Cuban cuisine
Villa La Mar.
Cárdenas. Matanzas
Phone: (53 45) 61-3910

El Mojito
Cuban cuisine
Hotel Breezes Varadero.
Cárdenas. Matanzas
Phone: (53 45) 66-7030

Ranchón El Compay
Cuban cuisine
Calle 54 e/ 1ra. y Playa.
Cárdenas. Matanzas
Phone: (53 45) 61-2460

El Nilo
Buffet restaurant
Oasis Tennis Centre.
Cárdenas. Matanzas
Phone: (53 45) 66-7380

Ranchón El Criollito
Cuban cuisine
Calle 1ra y 40.
Cárdenas. Matanzas
Phone: (53 45) 61-2180

El Paso
Light Meals
Hotel & Villas Tortuga.
Cárdenas. Matanzas
Phone: (53 45) 61-4747

Ranchón Playa Grill
Grill
Hotel Barceló Marina Palace.
Cárdenas. Matanzas
Phone: (53 45) 66-9966

El Paso
Light Meals
Ave. 1ra. y 7, Reparto Kawama.
Cárdenas. Matanzas

Ranchón Tropimar
Buffet restaurant
Hotel Barceló Solymar Beach
Resort. Cárdenas. Matanzas
Phone: (53 45) 61-4499

El Picante
Grill
Hotel Varadero Internacional.
Cárdenas. Matanzas
Phone: (53 45) 66-7038

Reflexión
Buffet restaurant
Hotel Meliá Las Antillas.
Cárdenas. Matanzas
Phone: (53 45) 668470

WHERE TO DINE
(VARADERO)

El Potro

International cuisine

Hotel Herradura.

Cárdenas. Matanzas

Phone: (53 45) 61-3703

Restaurante Buffet

Buffet restaurant

Hotel Breezes Varadero.

Cárdenas. Matanzas

Phone: (53 45) 66-7030

El Proel

Grill

Hotel Sol Sirenas-Coral.

Cárdenas. Matanzas

Phone: (53 45) 66-8070

Restaurante Chino

Asian cuisine

Calle 54 y 1ra.

Cárdenas. Matanzas

Phone: (53 45) 61-2460

El Rancho

Mexican cuisine

Hotel Tuxpan.

Cárdenas. Matanzas

Phone: (53 45) 66-7560

**Restaurante Especial
A la Carte**

International cuisine

Hotel Arenas Blancas.

Cárdenas. Matanzas

Phone: (53 45) 61-4450

El Ranchón

Light Meals

Hotel Taínos.

Cárdenas. Matanzas

Phone: (53 45) 66-8656

**Restaurantes de Pizzas
y Pastas**

Italian cuisine

Hotel Arenas Blancas.

Cárdenas. Matanzas

Phone: (53 45) 61-4450

El Ranchón

Grill

Hotel Cuatro Palmas.

Cárdenas. Matanzas

Phone: (53 45) 66-7040

Rizzolino

Italian cuisine

Hotel Kawama.

Cárdenas. Matanzas

Phone: (53 45) 61-4416

El Retiro

International cuisine

Calle 1ra. e/ 56 y 58, Parque
Josone. Cárdenas. Matanzas

Phone: (53 45) 66-7228

Salón de la Reina

International cuisine

Calle 1ra. e/ 25 y 26.

Cárdenas. Matanzas

Phone: (53 45) 66-7736

El Rodizio

International cuisine

Hotel Taínos.

Cárdenas. Matanzas

Phone: (53 45) 66-8656

Salón Violeta

Italian cuisine

Calle 44 y 1ra.

Cárdenas. Matanzas

Phone: (53 45) 61-2866

El Timonel

Buffet restaurant

Hotel Sol Sirenas-Coral.

Cárdenas. Matanzas

Phone: (53 45) 66-8070

Santa Clara

French cuisine

Hotel Varadero 1920.

Cárdenas. Matanzas

Phone: (53 45) 66-8288

El Toro

Red meat

Hotel Club Tropical.

Cárdenas. Matanzas

Phone: (53 45) 61-3915

Schooners

Fish and seafood

Hotel Meliá Las Antillas.

Cárdenas. Matanzas

Phone: (53 45) 668470

Fantasía

International cuisine

Hotel Brisas del Caribe.

Cárdenas. Matanzas

Phone: (53 45) 66-8030

Semi

Buffet restaurant

Hotel Club Puntarena.

Cárdenas. Matanzas

Phone: (53 45) 66-7125

Fuerteventura

International cuisine

Hotel Meliá Varadero.

Cárdenas. Matanzas

Phone: (53 45) 66-7013

WHERE TO DINE
(VARADERO)

Sirena
Light Meals
Villa La Mar.
Cárdenas. Matanzas
Phone: (53 45) 61-3910

Gran Canal
International cuisine
Hotel Kawama.
Cárdenas. Matanzas
Phone: (53 45) 61-4416

Sirocco
International cuisine
Hotel Sol Sirenas-Coral.
Cárdenas. Matanzas
Phone: (53 45) 66-8070

Grill
Grill
Hotel Brisas del Caribe.
Cárdenas. Matanzas
Phone: (53 45) 66-8030

Sol Cubano
Cuban cuisine
Hotel Sol Palmeras.
Cárdenas. Matanzas
Phone: (53 45) 66-7009

Grill Los Loritos
Grill
Hotel Arenas Doradas.
Cárdenas. Matanzas
Phone: (53 45) 66-8150

Sol y Arena
Cuban cuisine
Hotel Barceló Solymar Beach
Resort. Cárdenas. Matanzas
Phone: (53 45) 61-4499

Guaimaré
International cuisine
Ave. 1ra. e/ 26 y 27.
Cárdenas. Matanzas
Phone: (53 45) 61-1893

Splash
Grill
Villas Punta Blanca.
Cárdenas. Matanzas
Phone: (53 45) 66-8050

Guantanamera
Light Meals
Hotel Meliá Varadero.
Cárdenas. Matanzas
Phone: (53 45) 66-7013

Stella Di Mare
Italian cuisine
Hotel Paradisus Varadero.
Cárdenas. Matanzas
Phone: (53 45) 66-8700

Halong
Asian cuisine
Camino del Mar y 12.
Cárdenas. Matanzas
Phone: (53 45) 61-3787

**Taberna Dortmurder
Kneipe**
German cuisine
Camino del Mar e/ 13 y 14.
Cárdenas. Matanzas

Imperial
International cuisine
Hotel Los Delfines.
Cárdenas. Matanzas
Phone: (53 45) 66-7720

Taíno
Light Meals
Hotel Brisas del Caribe.
Cárdenas. Matanzas
Phone: (53 45) 66-8030

Islas
Buffet restaurant
Hotel Club Amigo Varadero.
Cárdenas. Matanzas
Phone: (53 45) 66-8243

Tihulam
Asian cuisine
Hotel Palma Real.
Cárdenas. Matanzas
Phone: (53 45) 61-4555

Kiki´s Club
Italian cuisine
Ave. 1ra. y 6.
Cárdenas. Matanzas
Phone: (53 45) 61-4115

Tocororo
Cuban cuisine
Hotel Tryp Península Varadero.
Cárdenas. Matanzas
Phone: (53 45) 66-8800

La Alhambra
Spanish cuisine
Hotel Paradisus Varadero.
Cárdenas. Matanzas
Phone: (53 45) 66-8700

Tortuga Grill
International cuisine
Hotel & Villas Tortuga.
Cárdenas. Matanzas
Phone: (53 45) 61-4747

WHERE TO DINE
(VARADERO)

La Arcada
International cuisine
Hotel Meliá Las Américas.
Cárdenas. Matanzas
Phone: (53 45) 66-7600

Trinidad
Grill
Hotel Meliá Varadero.
Cárdenas. Matanzas
Phone: (53 45) 66-7013

La Arcada
Buffet restaurant
Villas Punta Blanca.
Cárdenas. Matanzas
Phone: (53 45) 66-8050

Trinidad
Italian cuisine
Hotel Varadero 1920.
Cárdenas. Matanzas
Phone: (53 45) 66-8288

La Barbacoa
Red meat
Calle 1ra. y 64.
Cárdenas. Matanzas
Phone: (53 45) 66-7795

Tropimar
Fish and seafood
Hotel Barceló Solymar Beach
Resort. Cárdenas. Matanzas
Phone: (53 45) 61-4499

La Cabañita
International cuisine
Camino del Mar y 10.
Cárdenas. Matanzas
Phone: (53 45) 61-3787

Turey
International cuisine
Hotel Paradisus Varadero.
Cárdenas. Matanzas
Phone: (53 45) 66-8700

La Caleta
Italian cuisine
Hotel Meliá Las Américas.
Cárdenas. Matanzas
Phone: (53 45) 66-7600

Universal
International cuisine
Hotel Varadero Internacional.
Cárdenas. Matanzas
Phone: (53 45) 66-7038

La Campana
Cuban cuisine
Calle 1ra. e/ 56 y 58, Parque
Josone. Cárdenas. Matanzas
Phone: (53 45) 66-7228

Varadero
Buffet restaurant
Hotel Playa Alameda Varadero.
Cárdenas. Matanzas
Phone: (53 45) 66-8822

La Colina
International cuisine
Hotel Turquesa.
Cárdenas. Matanzas
Phone: (53 45) 66-8471

Varadero
Grill
Hotel Meliá Varadero.
Cárdenas. Matanzas
Phone: (53 45) 66-7013

La Esquina
Cuban cuisine
Calle 36 esq. a 1ra.
Cárdenas. Matanzas
Phone: (53 45) 61-4021

Varadero
Buffet restaurant
Hotel Bella Costa.
Cárdenas. Matanzas
Phone: (53 45) 66-7210

La Floresta
Light Meals
Hotel Playa Caleta.
Cárdenas. Matanzas
Phone: (53 45) 66-7120

Varadero
Buffet restaurant
Hotel Brisas del Caribe.
Cárdenas. Matanzas
Phone: (53 45) 66-8030

La Fondue
Casa del Queso Cubano
International cuisine
Ave. 1ra. e/ 62 y 63.
Cárdenas. Matanzas
Phone: (53 45) 66-7747

Varazul
Grill
Hotel Acuazul.
Cárdenas. Matanzas
Phone: (53 45) 66-7132

La Fontana
Italian cuisine
Villa Cuba Resort.
Cárdenas. Matanzas
Phone: (53 45) 66-8280

WHERE TO DINE
(HAVANA COLONIAL)

La Bodeguita del Medio
Cuban cuisine
Calle Empedrado No. 206 e/
San Ignacio y Cuba. La Habana
Vieja. La Habana
Phone: (53 7) 867-1374

A Prado y Neptuno
Italian cuisine
Paseo del Prado esq. a Neptuno.
La Habana Vieja. La Habana
Phone: (53 7) 860-9636

Al Medina
Arab cuisine
Calle Oficios No. 12 e/ Obispo
y Obrapía. La Habana Vieja.
Phone: (53 7) 867-1041

La Casa del Sandwich
Light Meals
Calle Empedrado e/ Tacón
y Ave. del Puerto. La Habana
Vieja. La Habana

Anacaona
International cuisine
Hotel Saratoga.
La Habana Vieja. La Habana
Phone: (53 7) 866-4317

La Casablanca
Light Meals
Calle Empedrado esq. a Tacón.
La Habana Vieja. La Habana
Phone: (53 7) 867-1027

Bar Cabaña
White meat
Calle Cuba No. 12.
La Habana Vieja. La Habana
Phone: (53 7) 860-5670

La Dichosa
Light Meals
Calle Obispo esq. a Compostela.
La Habana Vieja. La Habana

Bodegón "Onda"
Spanish cuisine
Hotel El Comendador.
La Habana Vieja. La Habana
Phone: (53 7) 867-1037

La Dominica
Italian cuisine
Calle O'Reilly No. 108
esquina a Mercaderes.
La Habana Vieja. La Habana
Phone: (53 7) 860-2918

Café del Oriente
International cuisine
Calle Oficios esq. a Amargura.
La Habana Vieja. La Habana
Phone: (53 7) 860-6686

La Eminencia
Baking-Pastry
Calle Jesús María esq. a
Compostela. La Habana Vieja.
La Habana

Café del Prado
Light Meals
Hotel Caribbean.
Centro Habana. La Habana
Phone: (53 7) 860-8233

La Floridana
International cuisine
Hotel Florida.
La Habana Vieja. La Habana
Phone: (53 7) 862-4127

Café La Logia
Light Meals
Capitolio de La Habana.
La Habana Vieja. La Habana

La Marina
International cuisine
Calle Teniente Rey esq. a Oficios.
La Habana Vieja. La Habana
Phone: (53 7) 862-9510

Café Taberna "Benny Moré"
International cuisine
Calle Mercaderes esq. a
Teniente Rey. La Habana Vieja.
La Habana
Phone: (53 7) 861-1637

La Mina
Cuban cuisine
Calle Obispo No. 106 esq. a
Oficios. La Habana Vieja.
La Habana
Phone: (53 7) 862-0216

Cantabria
International cuisine
Hotel Armadores de Santander.
La Habana Vieja. La Habana
Phone: (53 7) 862-8000

La Paella
Paellas
Hostal Valencia.
La Habana Vieja. La Habana
Phone: (53 7) 867-1037

Casa de las Infusiones
Light Meals
Calle Mercaderes e/ Obispo y
Obrapía. La Habana Vieja.
La Habana

WHERE TO DINE
(HAVANA COLONIAL)

Don Ricardo

International cuisine
Hotel Palacio O´Farrill.
La Habana Vieja. La Habana
Phone: (53 7) 860-5080

La Zaragozana

Spanish cuisine
Calle Monserrate No. 352.
La Habana Vieja. La Habana
Phone: (53 7) 867-1033

Doña Isabel

Light Meals
Calle Tacón No. 4.
La Habana Vieja. La Habana
Phone: (53 7) 867-1027

Las Columnas

Light Meals
Hotel Florida.
La Habana Vieja. La Habana
Phone: (53 7) 862-4127

El Baturro

Spanish cuisine
Calle Egido No. 661 e/ Jesús
María y Merced.
La Habana Vieja. La Habana
Phone: (53 7) 860-9078

**Las Palmeras de
Tallapiedra**

Cuban cuisine
Calle Tallapiedra e/ Alambique
y Diaria. La Habana Vieja.
Phone: (53 7) 862-8349

El Bosquecito

Calle O´Reilly esq. a San Ignacio
La Habana Vieja. La Habana
Phone: (53 7) 33-5670

Las Terrazas de Prado

Light Meals
Paseo del Prado esq. a Genios.
La Habana Vieja. La Habana
Phone: (53 7) 863-2814

El Colonial

International cuisine
Hotel Inglaterra.
La Habana Vieja. La Habana
Phone: (53 7) 860-8594

Los Cañones

Light Meals
Calle Cuba esq. a Peña Pobre.
La Habana Vieja. La Habana
Phone: (53 7) 860-5670

El Condado

International cuisine
Hotel Santa Isabel.
La Habana Vieja. La Habana
Phone: (53 7) 860-8201

Los Marinos

Light Meals
Calle Egido esq. a Merced.
La Habana Vieja. La Habana
Phone: (53 7) 862-1773

El Corojo

Light Meals
Hotel Conde de Villanueva.
La Habana Vieja. La Habana
Phone: (53 7) 862-9293

Los Marinos

Fish and seafood
Ave. del Puerto e/ Justiz y
Obrapía. La Habana Vieja.
La Habana
Phone: (53 7) 867-1402

El Floridita

Fish and seafood
Calle Obispo No. 557 esq. a
Moserrate. La Habana Vieja.
La Habana
Phone: (53 7) 867-1300

Los Portales

Cuban cuisine
Hotel Plaza. La Habana Vieja.
La Habana
Phone: (53 7) 860-8591

El Globo

Light Meals
Hotel Santa Isabel.
La Habana Vieja. La Habana
Phone: (53 7) 860-8201

Mediterráneo

International cuisine
Hotel Parque Central.
La Habana Vieja. La Habana
Phone: (53 7) 860-6627

El Laurel

Light Meals
Calle Obispo esq. a Compostela.
La Habana Vieja. La Habana

Park View

International cuisine
Hotel Park View.
La Habana Vieja. La Habana
Phone: (53 7) 861-3293

El Louvre

Light Meals
Hotel Inglaterra.
La Habana Vieja. La Habana
Phone: (53 7) 860-8594

WHERE TO DINE
(HAVANA COLONIAL)

Pastelería Francesa
Baking-Pastry
Paseo del Prado e/ San Rafael
y Neptuno. La Habana Vieja.
Phone: (53 7) 862-0739

El Mercurio
Diet-Vegetarian Cuisine
Lonja del Comercio, Plaza de
San Francisco de Asís.
La Habana Vieja. La Habana
Phone: (53 7) 860-6168

Plaza de Armas
International cuisine
Hotel Ambos Mundos.
La Habana Vieja. La Habana
Phone: (53 7) 860-9530

El Mesón de la Flota
Spanish cuisine
Calle Mercaderes No. 257 e/
Teniente Rey y Amargura.
La Habana Vieja. La Habana
Phone: (53 7) 863-3838

Prado y Animas
Light Meals
Prado y Animas.
La Habana Vieja. La Habana

El Naranjal
Ice Creams
Calle Obispo esq. a Cuba.
La Habana Vieja. La Habana
Phone: (53 7) 862-4127

Puerto de Sagua
Fish and seafood
Calle Egido No. 603 esq. a
Acosta. La Habana Vieja.
Phone: (53 7) 867-1026

La Dichosa
Light Meals
Calle Obispo esq. a Compostela.
La Habana Vieja. La Habana

Bodegón "Onda"
Spanish cuisine
Hotel El Comendador.
La Habana Vieja. La Habana
Phone: (53 7) 867-1037

La Dominica
Italian cuisine
Calle O´Reilly No. 108 esq. a
Mercaderes. La Habana Vieja.
La Habana
Phone: (53 7) 860-2918

Café del Oriente
International cuisine
Calle Oficios esq. a Amargura.
La Habana Vieja. La Habana
Phone: (53 7) 860-6686

La Eminencia
Baking-Pastry
Calle Jesús María esq. a
Compostela. La Habana Vieja.
La Habana

Café del Prado
Light Meals
Hotel Caribbean. Centro
Habana. La Habana
Phone: (53 7) 860-8233

La Floridana
International cuisine
Hotel Florida.
La Habana Vieja. La Habana
Phone: (53 7) 862-4127

Café La Logia
Light Meals
Capitolio de La Habana.
La Habana Vieja. La Habana

La Marina
International cuisine
Calle Teniente Rey esq. a Oficios.
La Habana Vieja. La Habana
Phone: (53 7) 862-9510

Café Taberna "Benny Moré"
International cuisine
Calle Mercaderes esq. a Teniente
Rey. La Habana Vieja.
La Habana
Phone: (53 7) 861-1637

La Mina
Cuban cuisine
Calle Obispo No. 106 esq. a
Oficios. La Habana Vieja.
La Habana
Phone: (53 7) 862-0216

Cantabria
International cuisine
Hotel Armadores de Santander.
La Habana Vieja. La Habana
Phone: (53 7) 862-8000

La Paella
Paellas
Hostal Valencia.
La Habana Vieja. La Habana
Phone: (53 7) 867-1037

Casa de las Infusiones
Light Meals
Calle Mercaderes e/ Obispo y
Obrapía. La Habana Vieja.
La Habana

WHERE TO DINE
(HAVANA COLONIAL)

El Paseo
International cuisine
Hotel Parque Central.
La Habana Vieja. La Habana
Phone: (53 7) 860-6627

Real Plaza
International cuisine
Hotel Plaza. La Habana Vieja.
La Habana
Phone: (53 7) 860-8591

El Patio
International cuisine
Calle San Ignacio No. 54,
Plaza de la Catedral.
La Habana Vieja. La Habana
Phone: (53 7) 867-1034

Roof Garden
International cuisine
Hotel Ambos Mundos.
La Habana Vieja. La Habana
Phone: (53 7) 860-9530

Entresuelo
Light Meals
Hostal Valencia. La Habana
Vieja. La Habana
Phone: (53 7) 867-1027

Salón Catedral
International cuisine
Hotel del Tejadillo.
La Habana Vieja. La Habana
Phone: (53 7) 863-7283

Fausto
Buffet restaurant
Hotel Plaza. La Habana Vieja.
La Habana
Phone: (53 7) 860-8591

San Carlos
Light Meals
Hotel del Tejadillo.
La Habana Vieja. La Habana
Phone: (53 7) 863-7283

Fornos Chá
Cuban cuisine
Calle Neptuno e/ Prado y
Consulado. La Habana Vieja.
La Habana
Phone: (53 7) 867-1032

San José
Light Meals
Calle Obispo e/ Mercaderes y
San Ignacio. La Habana Vieja.
Phone: (53 7) 860-9326

Fundación Havana Club
Light Meals
Ave. del Puerto No. 162.
La Habana Vieja. La Habana
Phone: (53 7) 861-1900

Santo Angel
International cuisine
Calle Teniente Rey esq. a San
Ignacio. La Habana Vieja.
Phone: (53 7) 861-1626

Gentiluomo
Italian cuisine
Calle Obispo esq. a Bernaza.
La Habana Vieja. La Habana
Phone: (53 7) 867-1300

Telégrafo
International cuisine
Hotel Telégrafo.
La Habana Vieja. La Habana
Phone: (53 7) 861-1010

Hanoi
Cuban cuisine
Calle Teniente Rey No. 507
esq. a Bernaza. La Habana Vieja.
La Habana
Phone: (53 7) 867-1029

Torrelavega
Light Meals
Calle Obrapía e/ Oficios y
Mercaderes. La Habana Vieja.
La Habana

Isamán
Light Meals
Ave. del Puerto y Empedrado.
La Habana Vieja. La Habana
Phone: (53 7) 867-1027

Vuelta Abajo
Cuban cuisine
Hotel Conde de Villanueva.
La Habana Vieja. La Habana
Phone: (53 7) 862-9293

La Azucena China
Asian cuisine
Calle Cienfuegos esq. a Monte.
La Habana Vieja. La Habana
Phone: (53 7) 860-9181

WHERE TO DINE
(HAVANA CITY)

1830
Cuban cuisine
Calle Calzada esq. a 20,
Plaza de la Revolución.
La Habana
Phone: (53 7) 55-3090

Habana Café
International cuisine
Hotel Meliá Cohiba. Plaza de
la Revolución. La Habana
Phone: (53 7) 33-3636

3ra. y 62
Light Meals
Calle 3ra. e/ 62 y 64,
Miramar. Playa. La Habana
Phone: (53 7) 204-0369

Habana Dentro
International cuisine
Hotel Lido. Centro Habana.
La Habana
Phone: (53 7) 867-1102

Acqua Marina
Light Meals
Hotel Deauville.
Centro Habana. La Habana
Phone: (53 7) 33-8812

Itapoa
International cuisine
Hotel Copacabana. Playa.
La Habana
Phone: (53 7) 204-1037

Al Fresco
Light Meals
Hotel Habana Riviera. Plaza de
la Revolución. La Habana
Phone: (53 7) 33-4051

Jardín de la Terraza
Grill
Hotel Lincoln.
Centro Habana. La Habana
Phone: (53 7) 33-8209

Allegro
Italian cuisine
Hotel Panamericano Resort.
La Habana del Este.
Phone: (53 7) 95-1010

Kasalta Sport Café
Italian cuisine
5ta. Ave. y 2, Miramar.
Playa. La Habana
Phone: (53 7) 204-0434

Amelia
International cuisine
Calle 3ra. e/ 78 y 80,
Miramar. Playa. La Habana

Kilimanjaro
International cuisine
Marina Hemingway Hotel y
Villas. Playa. La Habana
Phone: (53 7) 204-7628

Anacapri
Buffet restaurant
Hotel Capri. Plaza de la
Revolución. La Habana
Phone: (53 7) 33-3747

Kiosko Atlántico
Light Meals
Aparthotel Atlántico.
La Habana del Este.
La Habana
Phone: (53 7) 97-1203

Arcoiris
International cuisine
Hotel Bello Caribe. Playa.
La Habana
Phone: (53 7) 33-9906

L´Aiglon
International cuisine
Hotel Habana Riviera. Plaza de
la Revolución. La Habana
Phone: (53 7) 33-4051

Asador el Manantial
International cuisine
Calle 28 e/ 5ta. y 7ma.,
Miramar. Playa. La Habana
Phone: (53 7) 204-7410

La Arboleda
Light Meals
Hotel Nacional de Cuba. Plaza
de la Revolución. La Habana
Phone: (53 7) 33-3564

Atlántico
Italian cuisine
Hotel Atlántico.
La Habana del Este. La Habana
Phone: (53 7) 97-1085

La Bella Cubana
International cuisine
Hotel Meliá Habana. Playa.
La Habana
Phone: (53 7) 204-8500

Bazar 43
Light Meals
Calle 43 y 22. Playa.
La Habana
Phone: (53 7) 202-1872

WHERE TO DINE
(HAVANA CITY)

La Bonanza
International cuisine
Villa Los Pinos.
La Habana del Este. La Habana
Phone: (53 7) 97-1361

Bim Bom
Ice Creams
5ta. Ave. y 118, Miramar.
Playa. La Habana
Phone: (53 7) 33-9597

La Brasa
Grill
Hotel Meliá Cohiba. Plaza de
la Revolución. La Habana
Phone: (53 7) 33-3636

Bim Bom
Ice Creams
Calle 23 y Infanta, Vedado.
Plaza de la Revolución.
Phone: (53 7) 879-2892

La Casa del Pescador
Fish and seafood
Calle 5ta. e/ 440 y 442, Playa
Boca Ciega. La Habana del Este
Phone: (53 7) 96-3653

Bodegón Criollo
Cuban cuisine
Ave Monumental, La Cabaña.
La Habana del Este. La Habana
Phone: (53 7) 862-0617

La Casa del Tequila
Mexican cuisine
Hotel Neptuno-Tritón.
Playa. La Habana
Phone: (53 7) 204-1606

Boise
Light Meals
Comunidad Turística Marina
Hemingway. Playa. La Habana
Phone: (53 7) 204-7628

La Cascada
Buffet restaurant
Hotel Comodoro.
Playa. La Habana
Phone: (53 7) 204-5551

Bosque de La Habana
Ice Creams
Hotel Meliá Habana.
Playa. La Habana
Phone: (53 7) 204-8500

La Casona de 17
Cuban cuisine
Calle 17 No. 60, Vedado. Plaza
de la Revolución. La Habana
Phone: (53 7) 33-4529

Bugambil
Buffet restaurant
Hotel Mégano.
La Habana del Este. La Habana
Phone: (53 7) 97-1610

La Cecilia
Cuban cuisine
5ta. Ave. e/ 110 y 112,
Miramar. Playa. La Habana
Phone: (53 7) 204-1562

Burgui 23 y H
Light Meals
Calle 23 y H, Vedado.
Plaza de la Revolución.
Phone: (53 7) 33-4500

La Central
Light Meals
Calle Monte esq. a Belascoaín.
La Habana Vieja. La Habana

Burgui 26
Light Meals
Calle 26 e/ Kohly y 35, Nuevo
Vedado. Plaza de la Revolución.

La Divina Pastora
Fish and seafood
Ave Monumental, La Cabaña.
La Habana del Este. La Habana
Phone: (53 7) 860-8341

Burgui 5ta y 118
Light Meals
5ta. Ave. y 118, Miramar.
Playa. La Habana
Phone: (53 7) 33-9597

La Estancia
Cuban cuisine
Carretera de Vento km. 8,
Reparto Capdevila. Boyeros.
La Habana
Phone: (53 7) 33-8918

Burgui 5ta. y 98
Light Meals
5ta. Ave. y 98, Miramar.
Playa. La Habana
Phone: (53 7) 204-0788

La Estancia
International cuisine
Hotel Bello Caribe.
Playa. La Habana
Phone: (53 7) 33-9906

WHERE TO DINE
(HAVANA CITY)

Burgui América
Light Meals
Calle Galiano y Neptuno.
Centro Habana. La Habana
Phone: (53 7) 33-8430

La Ferminia
International cuisine
5ta. Ave. No. 18207, Reparto
Flores. Playa. La Habana
Phone: (53 7) 33-6786

Burgui Línea
Light Meals
Calle Línea y Paseo, Vedado.
Plaza de la Revolución.
La Habana

La Florentina
Italian cuisine
Hotel Capri. Plaza de la
Revolución. La Habana
Phone: (53 7) 33-3747

Café 42
Light Meals
Calle 5ta. A e/ 40 y 42,
Miramar. Playa. La Habana

La Floresta
International cuisine
Hotel Mariposa. La Lisa.
La Habana
Phone: (53 7) 204-9137

Café D´Porto
Italian cuisine
Hotel Copacabana. Playa.
La Habana
Phone: (53 7) 204-1037

La Fuente
Cuban cuisine
Calle 72 e/ 41 y 45.
Marianao. La Habana
Phone: (53 7) 267-1584

**Casa Club Horizontes
Atlántico**
International cuisine
Aparthotel Atlántico.
La Habana del Este.
Phone: (53 7) 97-1494

La Fuente
International cuisine
Calle 5ta. A e/ 40 y 42,
Miramar. Playa. La Habana
Phone: (53 7) 204-2372

Chef D´Oeuvre
French cuisine
Club Le Select, 5ta. Ave. y 30,
Miramar. Playa. La Habana
Phone: (53 7) 204-7410

La Giraldilla
International cuisine
Calle 222 e/ 37 y Autopista,
Reparto La Coronela. La Lisa.
Phone: (53 7) 33-6390

Chef Vedado
Buffet restaurant
Hotel Vedado. Plaza de la
Revolución. La Habana
Phone: (53 7) 33-4072

La Maison
International cuisine
Calle 16 e/ 7ma. y 9na.,
Miramar. Playa. La Habana
Phone: (53 7) 204-1543

Cojímar
Fish and seafood
Marina Tarará.
La Habana del Este.
Phone: (53 7) 97-1159

La Parrillada
Red meat
Hotel Neptuno-Tritón.
Playa. La Habana
Phone: (53 7) 204-1606

Colonial
International cuisine
Hotel Lincoln.
Centro Habana. La Habana
Phone: (53 7) 33-8209

La Pérgola
Italian cuisine
Calle 49-C y 28-A, Reparto
Kohly. Playa. La Habana
Phone: (53 7) 204-4990

Comedor de Aguiar
International cuisine
Hotel Nacional de Cuba.
Plaza de la Revolución.
La Habana
Phone: (53 7) 33-3564

La Piazza
Italian cuisine
Hotel Meliá Cohiba.
Plaza de la Revolución.
Phone: (53 7) 33-3636

Comodoro
International cuisine
Hotel Comodoro.
Playa. La Habana
Phone: (53 7) 204-5551

WHERE TO DINE
(HAVANA CITY)

La Picola Italia

Italian cuisine

Hotel Blau Club Arenal.

La Habana del Este.

Phone: (53 7) 97-1272

Concha y Cristina

Light Meals

Concha esq. a Cristina.

La Habana Vieja. La Habana

La Pradera

International cuisine

Hotel La Pradera. Playa.

Phone: (53 7) 33-7467

Coppelia

Ice Creams

Calle 23 esq. a L, Vedado.

Plaza de la Revolución.

La Rampa

Light Meals

Hotel Habana Libre Tryp.

Plaza de la Revolución.

Phone: (53 7) 33-4011

Coral Negro

International cuisine

Hotel Neptuno-Tritón. Playa.

Phone: (53 7) 204-1606

La Roca

International cuisine

Calle 21 esq. a M, Vedado.

Plaza de la Revolución.

Phone: (53 7) 33-4501

Costa Norte

International cuisine

Hotel Deauville. Centro Habana

Phone: (53 7) 33-8812

La Rueda

Cuban cuisine

Calle 294 e/ 181 y 187, Rpto.

El Chico. Boyeros. La Habana

Phone: (53 7) 45-3246

Cuatro Caminos

Light Meals

Calle Monte e/ Matadero y

Arroyo. La Habana Vieja.

Phone: (53 7) 860-9608

La Scala

Italian cuisine

Hotel Meliá Habana. Playa.

Phone: (53 7) 204-8500

Cubanitas 3ra. y 70

Light Meals

Calle 3ra. y 70, Miramar.

Playa. La Habana

Phone: (53 7) 204-2890

La Taberna del 1830

International cuisine

Calle Calzada esq. a 20, Vedado.

Plaza de la Revolución.

Phone: (53 7) 833-9907

Cubanitas Focsa

Light Meals

Calle 17 esq. a N, Bajos Edificio

Focsa, Vedado. Plaza de la

Revolución. La Habana

Phone: (53 7) 33-4499

La Tasca

Fish and seafood

Ave Monumental, La Cabaña.

La Habana del Este. La Habana

Phone: (53 7) 860-8341

Cubanitas Pavo Real

Light Meals

Calle 7ma. e/ 2 y 4, Miramar.

Playa. La Habana

Phone: (53 7) 204-2315

La Terraza

Grill

Hotel Meliá Habana.

Playa. La Habana

Phone: (53 7) 204-8500

Don Cangrejo

Fish and seafood

Calle 1ra. No. 1606,

Miramar. Playa. La Habana

Phone: (53 7) 204-4169

La Terraza de Cojímar

Fish and seafood

Calle Real No. 161, Cojímar.

La Habana del Este. La Habana

Phone: (53 7) 55-9232

Dona-Dona

Light Meals

5ta Ave. y 118, Miramar.

Playa. La Habana

Phone: (53 7) 33-9597

La Terraza di Roma

Italian cuisine

Hotel Comodoro.

Playa. La Habana

Phone: (53 7) 204-5551

Doñaneli

Baking-Pastry

Galerías de Paseo, Calle 1ra.

e/ Paseo y A, Vedado.

Plaza de la Revolución.

Phone: (53 7) 55-3170

WHERE TO DINE
(HAVANA CITY)

La Torre
International cuisine
Calle 17 No. 55, Edificio Focsa
piso 36, Vedado. Plaza de la
Revolución. La Habana
Phone: (53 7) 55-3088

Doñaneli
Baking-Pastry
Calle 182 e/ 13 y 15, Reparto
Siboney. Playa. La Habana
Phone: (53 7) 33-6452

La Veranda
Buffet restaurant
Hotel Nacional de Cuba. Plaza
de la Revolución. La Habana
Phone: (53 7) 33-3564

Doñaneli
Baking-Pastry
Calle 5ta.A y 42, Miramar.
Playa. La Habana

La Vicaria
International cuisine
5ta Ave. esq. a 180, Reparto
Flores. Playa. La Habana
Phone: (53 7) 33-9100

Dos Lunas
Buffet restaurant
Hotel Atlántico.
La Habana del Este.
La Habana
Phone: (53 7) 97-1085

La Yagruma
Light Meals
Hotel El Bosque.
Playa. La Habana
Phone: (53 7) 204-9232

El Abanico de Cristal
International cuisine
Hotel Meliá Cohiba.
Plaza de la Revolución.
Phone: (53 7) 33-3636

Las Antillas
Buffet restaurant
Hotel Habana Libre Tryp.
Plaza de la Revolución.
Phone: (53 7) 33-4011

El Acana
Light Meals
Hotel Bello Caribe.
Playa. La Habana
Phone: (53 7) 33-9906

Las Arenas
International cuisine
Villa Armonía Tarará.
La Habana del Este.
Phone: (53 7) 97-1616

El Aljibe
Cuban cuisine
Calle 7ma. e/ 24 y 26,
Miramar. Playa. La Habana
Phone: (53 7) 204-1583

Las Bulerías
Spanish cuisine
Calle L e/ 23 y 25, Vedado.
Plaza de la Revolución.
La Habana
Phone: (53 7) 832-3283

El Ancora
Grill
Hotel Atlántico.
La Habana del Este.
Phone: (53 7) 97-1085

Las Palmas
Buffet restaurant
Hotel Tropicoco.
La Habana del Este.
Phone: (53 7) 97-1371

El Bambú
Diet-Vegetarian Cuisine
Jardín Botánico Nacional.
Arroyo Naranjo. La Habana
Phone: (53 7) 44-8743

Las Ruinas
International cuisine
Calle 100 y Cortina de la Presa,
Parque Lenin. Arroyo Naranjo.
Phone: (53 7) 57-8286

El Barracón
Cuban cuisine
Hotel Habana Libre Tryp.
Plaza de la Revolución.
Phone: (53 7) 33-4011

Las Terrasitas
Light Meals
Villa Armonía Tarará.
La Habana del Este.
Phone: (53 7) 97-1616

El Bodegón del Este
Cuban cuisine
Calle 1ra. y 2da., Playa Boca
Ciega. La Habana del Este.
Phone: (53 7) 96-3089

Las Terrazas
International cuisine
Aparthotel Las Terrazas.
La Habana del Este.
Phone: (53 7) 97-1344

WHERE TO DINE
(HAVANA CITY)

El Brocal
Mexican cuisine
Calle 5ta. esq. a 500, Playa
Guanabo. La Habana del Este.
Phone: (53 7) 96-2892

Las Vistas
International cuisine
Villas Mirador del Mar.
La Habana del Este.
Phone: (53 7) 97-1354

El Chino
Asian cuisine
Vía Blanca km 18.
La Habana del Este.
Phone: (53 7) 97-1097

Le Roi
International cuisine
Hotel Chateau Miramar.
Playa. La Habana
Phone: (53 7) 204-1952

El Conejito
White meat
Calle M y 17, Vedado.
Plaza de la Revolución.
La Habana
Phone: (53 7) 832-4671

Los Doce Apóstoles
Cuban cuisine
Ave Monumental, La Cabaña.
La Habana del Este
Phone: (53 7) 860-8341

El Cortijo
Spanish cuisine
Hotel Vedado. Plaza de la
Revolución. La Habana
Phone: (53 7) 33-4072

Los Jardines de Tropicana
International cuisine
Calle 72 e/ 41 y 45.
Marianao. La Habana
Phone: (53 7) 267-1717

El Cotilo
Light Meals
Hotel Meliá Cohiba.
Plaza de la Revolución.
Phone: (53 7) 33-3636

Los Nísperos
Grill
Hotel Bello Caribe.
Playa. La Habana
Phone: (53 7) 33-9906

El Criollo
Cuban cuisine
Hotel Lincoln.
Centro Habana. La Habana
Phone: (53 7) 33-8209

Los Orishas
International cuisine
Calle Martí e/ Cruz Verde y
Lamas. Guanabacoa.
Phone: (53 7) 97-9510

El Dorado
International cuisine
Villa Bacuranao.
La Habana del Este.
Phone: (53 7) 65-7645

Mamá Inés
Cuban cuisine
Hotel Saint John´s.
Plaza de la Revolución.
Phone: (53 7) 33-3740

El Emperador
International cuisine
Calle 17 e/ M y N, Edificio Focsa,
Vedado. Plaza de la Revolución.
Phone: (53 7) 832-4998

Marakas
Light Meals
Calle O No. 206 e/ 23 y
Humboldt, Vedado. Plaza de
la Revolución. La Habana
Phone: (53 7) 33-3740

El Galeón
International cuisine
Aparthotel Atlántico.
La Habana del Este.
Phone: (53 7) 97-1203

Mi Casita de Coral
International cuisine
Ave. Las Terrazas Sur y Ave.
Las Banderas. La Habana del
Este. La Habana
Phone: (53 7) 97-1602

El Jardín
Light Meals
Hotel Kohly. Playa. La Habana
Phone: (53 7) 204-0240

Mi Cayito
Cuban cuisine
Laguna Itabo, Playa Santa María
del Mar. La Habana del Este.
Phone: (53 7) 97-1339

El Juvenil
Light Meals
Calle Monte No. 107.
La Habana Vieja. La Habana
Phone: (53 7) 860-9181

WHERE TO DINE
(HAVANA CITY)

Mi Patio
Italian cuisine
Hotel Kohly. Playa. La Habana
Phone: (53 7) 204-0240

El Lugar
International cuisine
Calle 49-C y 28-A, Reparto
Kohly. Playa. La Habana
Phone: (53 7) 204-4990

Mi Rinconcito
Italian cuisine
Villa Los Pinos.
La Habana del Este. La Habana
Phone: (53 7) 97-1361

El Mandarín
Asian cuisine
Calle 23 y M, Vedado. Plaza de
la Revolución. La Habana
Phone: (53 7) 832-0677

Mirador Habana
Grill
Hotel Habana Riviera. Plaza de
la Revolución. La Habana
Phone: (53 7) 33-4051

El Mesón de La Chorrera
Spanish cuisine
Malecón e/ 18 y 20, Vedado.
Plaza de la Revolución.
La Habana
Phone: (53 7) 833-4504

Miramar
Buffet restaurant
Hotel Meliá Habana.
Playa. La Habana
Phone: (53 7) 204-8500

El Mirador
International cuisine
Villas Mirador del Mar.
La Habana del Este. La Habana
Phone: (53 7) 97-1354

Monseigneur
International cuisine
Calle 21 esq. a 0, Vedado. Plaza
de la Revolución. La Habana
Phone: (53 7) 832-9884

El Náutico
Grill
Villas Mirador del Mar.
La Habana del Este. La Habana
Phone: (53 7) 97-1354

Montaña de Oro
Asian cuisine
Hotel Lincoln.
Centro Habana. La Habana
Phone: (53 7) 33-8209

El Nautilius
Light Meals
5ta Ave. y 152, Rpto.
Náutico. Playa. La Habana
Phone: (53 7) 33-05005

Náutico
Light Meals
Centro Comercial Náutico.
Playa. La Habana
Phone: (53 7) 33-6252

El Oasis
Light Meals
Paseo del Prado e/ Animas y
Trocadero. Centro Habana.
Phone: (53 7) 863-2122

Olímpico
International cuisine
Hotel Panamericano Resort.
La Habana del Este. La Habana
Phone: (53 7) 95-1010

El Palenque
Cuban cuisine
Ave. 17 e/ 174 y 190, Reparto
Siboney. Playa. La Habana

Pabellón del Tesoro
Asian cuisine
Comunidad Turística Marina
Hemingway. Playa. La Habana

El Patio
Light Meals
Calle 17 esq. M, Edificio Focsa,
Vedado. Plaza de la Revolución.
La Habana
Phone: (53 7) 33-4499

Panorama
International cuisine
Hotel Panorama.
Playa. La Habana
Phone: (53 7) 204-0100

El Patio de Quinta
International cuisine
Hotel Miramar.
Playa. La Habana
Phone: (53 7) 204-3584

Papa-Sam
Asian cuisine
Hotel Tropicoco.
La Habana del Este. La Habana
Phone: (53 7) 97-1371

WHERE TO DINE
(HAVANA CITY)

El Pedregal

International cuisine
Ave. 23 y 198. La Lisa.
La Habana
Phone: (53 7) 33-7832

Papa´s

Fish and seafood
Marina Hemingway.
Playa. La Habana
Phone: (53 7) 209-7920

El Polinesio

Asian cuisine
Hotel Habana Libre Tryp.
Plaza de la Revolución.
Phone: (53 7) 33-4011

Parrillada

Grill
Hotel La Pradera.
Playa. La Habana
Phone: (53 7) 33-7467

El Rancho

Cuban cuisine
Calle 140 y 19, Reparto
Cubanacán. Playa. La Habana
Phone: (53 7) 208-9346

Parrillada

Grill
Hotel Mariposa. La Lisa.
La Habana
Phone: (53 7) 204-9137

El Ranchón

Grill
Hotel Blau Club Arenal.
La Habana del Este.
Phone: (53 7) 97-1272

Parrillada

Grill
Hotel Comodoro.
Playa. La Habana
Phone: (53 7) 204-5551

El Ranchón

Cuban cuisine
5ta. Ave. esq. a 16,
Miramar. Playa. La Habana
Phone: (53 7) 204-1185

Parrillada La Caribeña

Cuban cuisine
Calle 7ma. esq. a 26,
Miramar. Playa. La Habana
Phone: (53 7) 204-2353

El Rápido "100 y 51"

Light Meals
Ave. 100 y 51.
Marianao. La Habana
Phone: (53 7) 267-1362

Pavo Real

Asian cuisine
Calle 7ma. No. 205 e/ 2 y 4,
Miramar. Playa. La Habana
Phone: (53 7) 204-2315

El Rápido "11 y 4"

Light Meals
Calle 4 e/ 11 y 13, Vedado.
Plaza de la Revolución.
Phone: (53 7) 33-4492

Pico Blanco

Grill
Hotel Saint John´s. Plaza de
la Revolución. La Habana
Phone: (53 7) 33-3740

El Rápido "114 y 39"

Light Meals
Calle 114 e/ 37 y 39.
Marianao. La Habana
Phone: (53 7) 267-1452

Pinomar

Light Meals
Villa Los Pinos.
La Habana del Este. La Habana
Phone: (53 7) 97-1361

El Rápido "15 y L"

Light Meals
Calle 15 e/ L y M, Vedado. Plaza
de la Revolución. La Habana
Phone: (53 7) 33-4497

Pizza Nova

Italian cuisine
Calle 17 esq. a 10, Vedado. Plaza
de la Revolución. La Habana

El Rápido "23 y 14"

Light Meals
Calle 23 esq. a 14, Vedado. Plaza
de la Revolución. La Habana
Phone: (53 7) 33-3992

Pizza Nova

Italian cuisine
Calle 3ra. esq. a 46,
Miramar. Playa. La Habana

El Rápido "3ra. y 10"

Light Meals
Calle 3ra. esq. a 10, Vedado.
Plaza de la Revolución.
La Habana
Phone: (53 7) 33-4716

WHERE TO DINE
(HAVANA CITY)

Pizza Nova La Cova
Italian cuisine
Marina Hemingway.
Playa. La Habana
Phone: (53 7) 204-6969

El Rápido "Camagüey"
Light Meals
Calle Galiano e/ Virtudes y
Concordia. Centro Habana.
La Habana
Phone: (53 7) 33-5622

Plaza Habana
Buffet restaurant
Hotel Meliá Cohiba. Plaza de
la Revolución. La Habana
Phone: (53 7) 33-3636

El Rápido "Casablanca"
Light Meals
Ave. 1ra. y 36,
Miramar. Playa. La Habana

Primavera
Buffet restaurant
Hotel Habana Riviera. Plaza de
la Revolución. La Habana
Phone: (53 7) 33-4051

El Rápido "Cibeles"
Light Meals
Calle N e/ 23 y 25, Vedado.
Plaza de la Revolución.
Phone: (53 7) 66-2368

Rancho Mi Hacienda
Cuban cuisine
Calzada de Justiz Km. 4 ½,
Campo Florido.
La Habana del Este. La Habana
Phone: (53 7) 96-4711

El Rápido "Dominica"
Light Meals
Vía Blanca Km. 13.
La Habana del Este.

Ranchón Caney
Grill
Hotel Tropicoco.
La Habana del Este.
Phone: (53 7) 97-1371

El Rápido "El Sol"
Light Meals
Calle 3ra. No. 340, Zona 1,
Alamar. La Habana del Este.
La Habana

Ranchón El Bajareque
Cuban cuisine
5ta. Ave. e/ 110 y 112,
Miramar. Playa. La Habana
Phone: (53 7) 204-1562

El Rápido "Faro de Guanabo"
Light Meals
Vía Blanca Km. 26.
La Habana del Este.
Phone: (53 7) 96- 2770

Ranchón Hatuey
Cuban cuisine
Carretera de Vento km. 8,
Reparto Capdevila. Boyeros.
La Habana
Phone: (53 7) 33-8918

El Rápido "Faro Infanta"
Light Meals
Calle Infanta esq. a San Rafael.
Centro Habana. La Habana
Phone: (53 7) 33-5951

Rincón Criollo
Cuban cuisine
Hotel Panamericano Resort.
La Habana del Este. La Habana
Phone: (53 7) 95-1010

El Rápido "Havana in Bond"
Light Meals
Valle de Berroa.
La Habana del Este. La Habana
Phone: (53 7) 66-9859

Rossini
Italian cuisine
Calle 5ta. A e/ 40 y 42,
Miramar. Playa. La Habana
Phone: (53 7) 204-2450

El Rápido "La Estrella"
Light Meals
Vía Blanca y Durege, Rpto.
Santos Suárez. Diez de Octubre.
La Habana

Salón Cristal
Buffet restaurant
Hotel Neptuno-Tritón.
Playa. La Habana
Phone: (53 7) 204-1606

El Rápido "La Palma"
Light Meals
Calle Porvenir y Georgia.
Arroyo Naranjo. La Habana

San Remo
Grill
Ave. 6ta. y 1ra., Playa Boca
Ciega. La Habana del Este.
La Habana
Phone: (53 7) 96-3068

WHERE TO DINE
(HAVANA CITY)

El Rápido
"La Primera del Cerro"
Light Meals
Calle Santa Catalina y Vento.
Cerro. La Habana
Phone: (53 7) 880-3192

Shanghai
Asian cuisine
Calle 7ma. esq. a 26,
Miramar. Playa. La Habana
Phone: (53 7) 204-2353

El Rápido "Mantilla"
Light Meals
Calzada Managua y Progreso.
Arroyo Naranjo. La Habana

Snack bar Grill
Light Meals
Hotel Miramar.
Playa. La Habana
Phone: (53 7) 204-3584

El Rápido
"Rincón Español"
Light Meals
Calle Ayestarán y Requena.
Plaza de la Revolución.
La Habana

Sylvain
Baking-Pastry
Calle Línea No. 951, Vedado.
Plaza de la Revolución.
La Habana

El Rápido "Sevillana"
Light Meals
Calle Zapata esq. a 26. Plaza de
la Revolución. La Habana
Phone: (53 7) 33-4495

Sylvain
Baking-Pastry
Calle 19 No. 3605, Miramar.
Playa. La Habana

El Rápido "Sierra Maestra"
Light Meals
Calle 1ra. e/ 0 y 2, Miramar.
Playa. La Habana
Phone: (53 7) 204-2268

Tapatío
Mexican cuisine
Hotel Panamericano Resort.
La Habana del Este. La Habana
Phone: (53 7) 95-1010

El Rápido "Ultra"
Light Meals
Calle Reina Nro. 109.
Centro Habana. La Habana
Phone: (53 7) 66-9222

Taramar
Fish and seafood
Vía Blanca km 18.
La Habana del Este. La Habana
Phone: (53 7) 97-1097

El Roble
International cuisine
Villa Armonía Tarará.
La Habana del Este. La Habana
Phone: (53 7) 97-1616

Terracita
Grill
Hotel Blau Club Arenal.
La Habana del Este. La Habana
Phone: (53 7) 97-1272

El Toro
Red meat
Hotel Panamericano Resort.
La Habana del Este. La Habana
Phone: (53 7) 95-2866

Terraza Habana
Light Meals
Ave. 47, Rpto. Kohly.
Playa. La Habana
Phone: (53 7) 203-6523

El Toro
Red meat
Hotel Saint John´s.
Plaza de la Revolución.
Phone: (53 7) 33-3740

Tocororo
International cuisine
Calle 18 y 3ra., Miramar.
Playa. La Habana
Phone: (53 7) 204-2209

Fiat
Light Meals
Malecón e/ Marina y Príncipe.
Centro Habana. La Habana
Phone: (53 7) 33-5827

Tropical
International cuisine
Hotel Colina. Plaza de la
Revolución. La Habana
Phone: (53 7) 33-4071

Fiesta
Spanish cuisine
Residencial Marina Hemingway.
Playa. La Habana
Phone: (53 7) 209-7917

WHERE TO DINE
(HAVANA CITY)

Tropical
International cuisine
Hotel Panamericano Resort.
La Habana del Este.
Phone: (53 7) 95-1010

Finca Guanabito
Cuban cuisine
Carretera de Jústiz km. 4,
Campo Florido.
La Habana del Este.
Phone: (53 7) 96-4610

Trópico
International cuisine
Hotel Kohly. Playa. La Habana
Phone: (53 7) 204-0240

Flores
Light Meals
Calle 176 e/ 1ra. y 5ta., Reparto
Flores. Playa. La Habana
Phone: (53 7) 33-6512

Tucán
Buffet restaurant
Hotel Copacabana.
Playa. La Habana
Phone: (53 7) 204-1037

Gambina
Italian cuisine
Calle 7ma. esq. a 26,
Miramar. Playa. La Habana
Phone: (53 7) 204-9662

Gato Tuerto
International cuisine
Calle O e/ 17 y 19, Vedado.
Plaza de la Revolución.
La Habana
Phone: (53 7) 66-2224

Victoria
International cuisine
Hotel Victoria. Plaza de la
Revolución. La Habana
Phone: (53 7) 33-3510

Gaviota
International cuisine
Aparthotel Atlántico.
La Habana del Este.
Phone: (53 7) 97-1203

Villa Diana
International cuisine
Calle 49 y 28-A, Reparto
Kohly. Playa. La Habana
Phone: (53 7) 202-7670

Gaviota
International cuisine
Hotel Blau Club Arenal.
La Habana del Este.
Phone: (53 7) 97-1272

Vuelta al Mundo
International cuisine
Hotel Miramar. Playa.
Phone: (53 7) 204-3584

Wakamba
International cuisine
Calle O e/ 23 y 25, Vedado.
Plaza de la Revolución.
Phone: (53 7) 878-4526

Habana
Light Meals
Hotel Vedado. Plaza de la
Revolución. La Habana
Phone: (53 7) 33-4072

Yara
Italian cuisine
Aparthotel Las Terrazas.
La Habana del Este.
Phone: (53 7) 97-1344

Turquino
International cuisine
Hotel Saint John´s. Plaza de
la Revolución. La Habana
Phone: (53 7) 33-3740

Guanabo Club
Cuban cuisine
Calle 468 e/ 13 y 15, Playa
Guanabo. La Habana del Este.
La Habana
Phone: (53 7) 96-2884

WHERE TO DINE
(SANTIAGO DE CUBA)

Alondra
Ice Creams
Ave. Garzón No. 398 e/ 5ta. y
6ta., Reparto Santa Bárbara.
Santiago de Cuba

La Fontana
Italian cuisine
Hotel Meliá Santiago de Cuba.
Santiago de Cuba
Phone: (53 22) 687-070

Baconao
Buffet restaurant
Hotel Bucanero.
Santiago de Cuba
Phone: (53 22) 68-6363

La Isabelica
International cuisine
Hotel Meliá Santiago de Cuba.
Santiago de Cuba
Phone: (53 22) 687-070

Balcón de Santiago
International cuisine
Motel Rancho Club.
Santiago de Cuba
Phone: (53 22) 63-3202

La Punta
Cuban cuisine
Carretera Baconao km. 22 ½,
La Punta. Santiago de Cuba

Barbecue
Grill
Hotel Carisol-Los Corales.
Santiago de Cuba
Phone: (53 22) 635-6150

La Teressina
Italian cuisine
Calle Aguilera e/ Calvario
y Reloj. Santiago de Cuba
Phone: (53 22) 65-2205

Costa Sol
Light Meals
Hotel Balcón del Caribe.
Santiago de Cuba
Phone: (53 22) 691-506

La Terraza
Light Meals
Hotel Casa Granda.
Santiago de Cuba
Phone: (53 22) 68-6600

Cupey
Buffet restaurant
Hotel Sierra Mar. Guamá.
Santiago de Cuba
Phone: (53 22) 62-6319

Lambada
Buffet restaurant
Hotel Carisol-Los Corales.
Santiago de Cuba
Phone: (53 22) 635-6150

Don Antonio
Cuban cuisine
Calle Aguilera e/ Calvario
y Reloj. Santiago de Cuba
Phone: (53 22) 65-2205

Las Acacias
International cuisine
Villa Santiago de Cuba.
Santiago de Cuba
Phone: (53 22) 64 1368

Doñaneli
Baking-Pastry
Calle 15 y 4, Reparto Vista
Alegre. Santiago de Cuba
Phone: (53 22) 64-1869

Las Américas
Light Meals
Hotel Las Américas.
Santiago de Cuba
Phone: (53 22) 64-2011

El Caney
International cuisine
Hacienda El Caney.
Santiago de Cuba
Phone: (53 22) 68-7134

Las Américas
Buffet restaurant
Hotel Las Américas.
Santiago de Cuba
Phone: (53 22) 64-2011

El Cayo
Fish and seafood
Cayo Granma, Bahía de Santiago
de Cuba. Santiago de Cuba
Phone: (53 22) 69-0109

Las Caletas
International cuisine
Hotel Balcón del Caribe.
Santiago de Cuba
Phone: (53 22) 691-506

El Colmadito
Light Meals
Hotel Meliá Santiago de Cuba.
Santiago de Cuba
Phone: (53 22) 687-070

WHERE TO DINE
(SANTIAGO DE CUBA)

Las Columnitas
Light Meals
Calle San Félix y Callejón del
Carmen. Santiago de Cuba
Phone: (53 22) 68-6028

El Criollo
Grill
Hotel Meliá Santiago de Cuba.
Santiago de Cuba
Phone: (53 22) 687-070

Leningrado
Buffet restaurant
Hotel San Juan.
Santiago de Cuba
Phone: (53 22) 68-7200

El Mirador
Light Meals
Carretera de Baconao,
Sigua. Santiago de Cuba

Los Galeones
Buffet restaurant
Hotel Sierra Mar. Guamá.
Santiago de Cuba
Phone: (53 22) 62-6160

El Morro
Cuban cuisine
Carretera del Morro Km. 8½.
Santiago de Cuba
Phone: (53 22) 68-7151

Los Vitrales
International cuisine
Hotel Versalles.
Santiago de Cuba
Phone: (53 22) 69-1016

El Panalito
International cuisine
Calle Manduley esq. a General
Cebreco, Reparto Vista Alegre.
Santiago de Cuba
Phone: (53 22) 64-1651

Marinero
Fish and seafood
Hotel Carisol-Los Corales.
Santiago de Cuba
Phone: (53 22) 635-6150

El Ranchón
Light Meals
Hotel Costa Morena.
Santiago de Cuba
Phone: (53 22) 635- 6126

Matamoros
Cuban cuisine
Calle Calvario e/ Enramada
y Aguilera. Santiago de Cuba

El Ranchón
Cuban cuisine
Hotel El Saltón. Tercer Frente.
Santiago de Cuba
Phone: (53 225) 6492

Orquídea
International cuisine
Hotel Costa Morena.
Santiago de Cuba
Phone: (53 22) 635- 6126

El Rodeo
Cuban cuisine
Carretera de Baconao, Barrio
Oasis. Santiago de Cuba

Parrillada
Grill
Hotel Bucanero.
Santiago de Cuba
Phone: (53 22) 68-6363

El Toro
Red meat
Hotel Las Américas.
Santiago de Cuba
Phone: (53 22) 642-011

Paso Doble
Buffet restaurant
Hotel Carisol-Los Corales.
Santiago de Cuba
Phone: (53 22) 635-6150

Finca El Porvenir
Cuban cuisine
Carretera de Baconao km. 18,
Alturas del río Juraguá.
Santiago de Cuba

Pavo Real
International cuisine
Autopista km. 1 ½.
Santiago de Cuba
Phone: (53 22) 64-1071

Gran Piedra
International cuisine
Motel Gran Piedra.
Santiago de Cuba
Phone: (53 22) 686147

Roof Garden
Buffet restaurant
Hotel Casa Granda.
Santiago de Cuba
Phone: (53 22) 68-6600

WHERE TO DINE
(SANTIAGO DE CUBA)

Joturo
International cuisine
Hotel Sierra Mar. Guamá.
Santiago de Cuba
Phone: (53 22) 629110

San Juan
Light Meals
Hotel San Juan.
Santiago de Cuba
Phone: (53 22) 68-7200

Kiam Sand
Asian cuisine
Carretera de Ciudamar km. 4 ½
y Entronque de Punta Gorda.
Santiago de Cuba
Phone: (53 22) 69-1889

Sitio de Compay Segundo
Cuban cuisine
Calle Montenegro s/n,
Siboney. Santiago de Cuba

La Casa de Rolando
Cuban cuisine
Carrtera Baconao km. 53.
Santiago de Cuba

Tratoria
Italian cuisine
Hotel Carisol-Los Corales.
Santiago de Cuba
Phone: (53 22) 635-6150

La Casona
Buffet restaurant
Hotel Meliá Santiago de Cuba.
Santiago de Cuba
Phone: (53 22) 687-070

Tropicana Santiago
International cuisine
Autopista Nacional km. 1 ½.
Santiago de Cuba
Phone: (53 22) 64-3036

La Cecilia
Cuban cuisine
Carretera a Ciudamar km. 4.
Santiago de Cuba
Phone: (53 22) 69-1889

Versalles
Grill
Hotel Versalles.
Santiago de Cuba
Phone: (53 22) 691-016

Tocororo
International cuisine
Ave. Manduley No. 159, Reparto
Vista Alegre. Santiago de Cuba
Phone: (53 22) 64-1369

La Cascada
Light Meals
Hotel El Saltón. Tercer Frente.
Santiago de Cuba
Phone: (53 225) 6492

La Ceiba
Cuban cuisine
Hotel San Juan.
Santiago de Cuba
Phone: (53 22) 68-7200

Zunzún
International cuisine
Ave. Manduley No. 159 e/ 5ta.
y 7ma., Reparto Vista Alegre.
Santiago de Cuba
Phone: (53 22) 641-528

WHERE TO DINE
(HOLGUÍN)

Acuario Cayo Naranjo
Fish and seafood
Carretera Guardalavaca km. 54.
Rafael Freyre. Holguín
Phone: (53 24) 30-132

La Ceiba
Buffet restaurant
Hotel Paradisus Río de Oro.
Rafael Freyre. Holguín
Phone: (53 24) 3-0090

Arenas Nuevas
Light Meals
Villa Don Lino.
Rafael Freyre. Holguín
Phone: (53 24) 3-0259

La Floresta
International cuisine
Villa El Cocal. Holguín
Phone: (53 24) 46-1902

Atabey
Buffet restaurant
Hotel Atlántico-Guardalavaca.
Banes. Holguín
Phone: (53 24) 3-0195

La Foresta
Italian cuisine
Hotel Occidental Grand Playa
Turquesa. Rafael Freyre.
Holguín

Bucanero
Mediterranean cuisine
Hotel Occidental Grand Playa
Turquesa. Rafael Freyre.
Holguín

La Guira
International cuisine
Villa Cayo Saetía.
Mayarí. Holguín
Phone: (53 24) 96900

Carabela
International cuisine
Hotel Sol Río de Luna y Mares.
Rafael Freyre. Holguín
Phone: (53 24) 3-0030

La Hacienda
Buffet restaurant
Hotel Occidental Grand Playa
Turquesa. Rafael Freyre.
Holguín

Casa Criolla
Cuban cuisine
Playa Guardalavaca.
Banes. Holguín

La Higuana
Buffet restaurant
Villa Cayo Saetía.
Mayarí. Holguín
Phone: (53 24) 96900

Colombo
Cuban cuisine
Parque Nacional Cristóbal
Colón, Cayo Bariay. Rafael
Freyre. Holguín

La Laguna
Grill
Hotel Paradisus Río de Oro.
Rafael Freyre. Holguín
Phone: (53 24) 30090

Colón
Buffet restaurant
Hotel Sol Río de Luna y Mares.
Rafael Freyre. Holguín
Phone: (53 24) 3-0030

La Niña
Light Meals
Hotel Sol Río de Luna y Mares.
Rafael Freyre. Holguín
Phone: (53 24) 3-0030

Compaygallo
Cuban cuisine
Carretera Guardalavaca km. 3.
Banes. Holguín
Phone: (53 24) 3-0132

La Pinta
Diet-Vegetarian Cuisine
Hotel Sol Río de Luna y Mares.
Rafael Freyre. Holguín
Phone: (53 24) 3-0030

Conuco de Mongo Viña
Cuban cuisine
Bahía de Naranjo.
Rafael Freyre. Holguín
Phone: (53 24) 30-915

La Terraza
International cuisine
Hotel Atlántico-Guardalavaca.
Banes. Holguín
Phone: (53 24) 3-0180

Conuco´s
Grill
Hotel Playa Costa Verde.
Rafael Freyre. Holguín
Phone: (53 24) 3-0520

WHERE TO DINE
(HOLGUÍN)

La Trattoria
Italian cuisine
Hotel Guardalavaca. Banes.
Phone: (53 24) 3-0218

El Ancla
Fish and seafood
Cayo Bariay. Rafael Freyre.
Phone: (53 24) 30-237

La Turquesa
Buffet restaurant
Hotel Guardalavaca. Banes.
Phone: (53 24) 3-0218

El Bohío
Cuban cuisine
Hotel Paradisus Río de Oro.
Rafael Freyre. Holguín
Phone: (53 24) 3-0090

El Cayuelo
Fish and seafood
Playa Guardalavaca. Banes.
Phone: (53 24) 30-422

Las Arcadas
Buffet restaurant
Hotel Atlántico-Guardalavaca.
Banes. Holguín
Phone: (53 24) 3-0180

Galileo
Cuban cuisine
Hotel Sol Río de Luna y Mares.
Rafael Freyre. Holguín
Phone: (53 24) 3-0030

II Ponticello
Hotel Blau Costa Verde.
Rafael Freyre. Holguín
Phone: (53 24) 3-0510

El Delfín
Fish and seafood
Playa Guardalavaca.
Banes. Holguín

Las Carabelas de Colón
Fish and seafood
Cayo Bariay. Rafael Freyre.
Holguín

El Framboyan
Fish and seafood
Playa Guardalavaca.
Banes. Holguín

Lucy´s
Light Meals
Hotel Playa Costa Verde.
Rafael Freyre. Holguín
Phone: (53 24) 3-0520

El Jagüey
White meat
Playa Guardalavaca.
Banes. Holguín

Mar Azul
Buffet restaurant
Villa Don Lino. Rafael Freyre.
Phone: (53 24) 3-0259

El Patio
International cuisine
Hotel Paradisus Río de Oro.
Rafael Freyre. Holguín
Phone: (53 24) 3-0090

Mar y Sol
International cuisine
Hotel Blau Costa Verde.
Rafael Freyre. Holguín
Phone: (53 24) 3-0510

El Patio
Fish and seafood
Hotel Guardalavaca. Banes.
Phone: (53 24) 30-218

Martino´s
Italian cuisine
Hotel Playa Costa Verde.
Rafael Freyre. Holguín
Phone: (53 24) 3-0520

El Toto
Light Meals
Playa Guardalavaca.
Banes. Holguín

Munahana
Asian cuisine
Hotel Playa Costa Verde.
Rafael Freyre. Holguín
Phone: (53 24) 3-0520

El Uvero
International cuisine
Playa Guardalavaca.
Banes. Holguín

Pizza Nova
Italian cuisine
Playa Guardalavaca. Banes.
Phone: (53 24) 30-137

El Zaguán
Buffet restaurant
Hotel Guardalavaca. Banes.
Phone: (53 24) 30-218

Restaurante Buffet
Buffet restaurant
Hotel Playa Costa Verde.
Rafael Freyre. Holguín
Phone: (53 24) 3-0520

WHERE TO DINE
(CAYO LARGO DEL SUR)

El Espigón
Fish and seafood
Villa Lindamar.
Isla de la Juventud
Phone: (53 45) 248 111

Los Quelonios
Cuban cuisine
Hotel Sol Pelícano.
Isla de la Juventud
Phone: (53 45) 248-333

El Gavilán
Italian cuisine
Villa Iguana.
Isla de la Juventud
Phone: (53 45) 248-111

Merlin Azul
Buffet restaurant
Villa Capricho.
Isla de la Juventud
Phone: (53 45) 248-111

Entre Mares
International cuisine
Hotel Sol Pelícano.
Isla de la Juventud
Phone: (53 45) 248-333

Olazul
Buffet restaurant
Hotel Barceló Cayo Largo Beach
Resort. Isla de la Juventud
Phone: (53 45) 248-080

La Piazzoletta
Italian cuisine
Villa Coral. Isla de la Juventud
Phone: (53 45) 248-111

Opalino
International cuisine
Hotel Barceló Cayo Largo Beach
Resort. Isla de la Juventud
Phone: (53 45) 248-080

La Yana
Italian cuisine
Hotel Sol Pelícano.
Isla de la Juventud
Phone: (53 45) 248-333

Ranchón Cayo Rico
International cuisine
Marina Cayo Largo del Sur.
Isla de la Juventud

Las Dunas
Buffet restaurant
Hotel Sol Cayo Largo.
Isla de la Juventud
Phone: (53 45) 248-260

Ranchón Sirena
International cuisine
Marina Cayo Largo del Sur.
Isla de la Juventud

Las Trinas
International cuisine
Hotel Sol Cayo Largo.
Isla de la Juventud
Phone: (53 45) 248-260

Solazul
Light Meals
Hotel Sol Cayo Largo.
Isla de la Juventud
Phone: (53 45) 248-260

Lindamar
Buffet restaurant
Villa Lindamar.
Isla de la Juventud
Phone: (53 45) 248-111

Taberna del Pirata
International cuisine
Marina Cayo Largo del Sur.
Isla de la Juventud

Lindarena
Cuban cuisine
Hotel Sol Cayo Largo.
Isla de la Juventud
Phone: (53 45) 248-260

Velamar
Cuban cuisine
Hotel Barceló Cayo Largo Beach
Resort. Isla de la Juventud
Phone: (53 45) 248-080

Los Canarreos
International cuisine
Hotel Isla del Sur.
Isla de la Juventud
Phone: (53 45) 248-111

Zun Zun
Light Meals
Hotel Sol Pelícano.
Isla de la Juventud
Phone: (53 45) 248-333

WHERE TO DINE
(TRINIDAD)

1514

Buffet restaurant

Hotel Trinidad del Mar.

Trinidad. Sancti Spiritus

Phone: (53 41) 96234

Los Cobos

Grill

Hotel Trinidad del Mar.

Trinidad. Sancti Spiritus

Phone: (53 41) 96234

Arrecife

Buffet restaurant

Hotel Costasur.

Trinidad. Sancti Spiritus

Phone: (53 419) 6174

Ma´ Dolores

Cuban cuisine

Finca Ma´ Dolores.

Trinidad. Sancti Spiritus

Phone: (53 419) 6481

Bahía de Casilda

Buffet restaurant

Hotel Ancón.

Trinidad. Sancti Spiritus

Phone: (53 419) 6120

Manacas-Iznaga

Cuban cuisine

Carretera de Sancti Spíritus Km.

12, Valle de Los Ingenios.

Trinidad. Sancti Spiritus

Phone: (53 419) 7241

El Pescador

Grill

Hotel Ancón. Trinidad.

Sancti Spiritus

Phone: (53 419) 6120

Caucobú

International cuisine

Hotel Las Cuevas.

Trinidad. Sancti Spiritus

Phone: (53 419) 6133

Olaya

Italian cuisine

Hotel Ancón. Trinidad.

Sancti Spiritus

Phone: (53 419) 6120

Don Antonio

International cuisine

Calle Gustavo Izquierdo

No. 118. Trinidad.

Sancti Spiritus

Phone: (53 419) 3198

Plaza Mayor

International cuisine

Calle Ruben Martínez Villena

esq. a Francisco J. Zerquera.

Trinidad. Sancti Spiritus

Phone: (53 419) 3180

El Jigüe

White meat

Calle Rubén Martínez Villena

No. 70. Trinidad. Sancti Spiritus

Phone: (53 419) 4315

Plaza Santa Ana

International cuisine

Calle Santo Domingo y Santa

Ana. Trinidad. Sancti Spiritus

Phone: (53 419) 3523

Ranchón La Boca

Fish and seafood

Playa La Boca. Trinidad.

Sancti Spiritus

Hacienda Los Molinos

Cuban cuisine

Carretera Sancti Spíritus km. 35.

Trinidad. Sancti Spiritus

Ruinas de Lleonci

International cuisine

Calle Gustavo Izquierdo No. 114.

Trinidad. Sancti Spiritus

Phone: (53 419) 3198

Las Conchas

Light Meals

Hotel Ancón. Trinidad.

Sancti Spiritus

Phone: (53 419) 6120

Trinidad Colonial

International cuisine

Calle Maceo No. 402.

Trinidad. Sancti Spiritus

Phone: (53 419) 3873

Lina

Italian cuisine

Hotel Costasur.

Trinidad. Sancti Spiritus

Phone: (53 419) 6174

Yara

International cuisine

Hotel La Ronda.

Trinidad. Sancti Spiritus

Phone: (53 419) 4011

WHERE TO DINE
(SOROA, LAS TERRAZAS & VIÑALES)

Buenavista

Cuban cuisine
Complejo Las Terrazas.
Candelaria. Artemisa

Moka

Cuban cuisine
Hotel Moka.
Candelaria. Artemisa
Phone: (53 82) 778600

Casa del Campesino

Cuban cuisine
Complejo Las Terrazas.
Candelaria. Artemisa

Parrillada

Grill
Hotel Moka.
Candelaria. Artemisa
Phone: (53 82) 778600

Castillo

Cuban cuisine
Villa Soroa.
Candelaria. Artemisa
Phone: (53 85) 2122

Rancho Curujey

Cuban cuisine
Complejo Las Terrazas.
Candelaria. Artemisa

Centro

International cuisine
Villa Soroa. Candelaria.
Phone: (53 85) 2122

La Terraza

Buffet restaurant
Hotel La Ermita. Viñales.
Phone: (53 8) 93-6071

Salto

Cuban cuisine
Villa Soroa. Candelaria.
Phone: (53 85) 2122

Fonda de Mercedes

Cuban cuisine
Complejo Las Terrazas.
Candelaria. Artemisa

Casa de Don Tomás

Cuban cuisine
Valle de Viñales. Viñales.
Pinar del Río
Phone: (53 8) 79-3114

Las Arcadas

Cuban cuisine
Hotel Rancho San Vicente.
Viñales. Pinar del Río
Phone: (53 8) 93-6201

Casa del Marisco

Fish and seafood
Carretera a Puerto Esperanza
km. 38. Viñales. Pinar del Río

Mirador Valle de Viñales

Carretera a Viñales km. 25.
Viñales. Pinar del Río
Phone: (53 8) 79-3205

Cueva del Indio

Cuban cuisine
Carretera a Puerto Esperanza
km. 38. Viñales. Pinar del Río
Phone: (53 8) 79-3202

Vitral

International cuisine
Hotel Los Jazmines. Viñales.
Phone: (53 8) 93-6205

Mural de la Prehistoria

Cuban cuisine
Valle de Viñales. Viñales.
Pinar del Río
Phone: (53 8) 79-3394

Cuevas de Viñales

Cuban cuisine
Carretera a Puerto Esperanza
km. 36. Viñales. Pinar del Río
Phone: (53 8) 79-3203

Ranchón San Vicente

Cuban cuisine
Carretera a Puerto Esperanza
km. 38. Viñales. Pinar del Río
Phone: (53 82) 79-3200

Fausto Azul

Grill
Hotel La Ermita.
Viñales. Pinar del Río
Phone: (53 8) 93-6071

Restaurante a la carta

Cuban cuisine
Villa Aguas Claras.
Viñales. Pinar del Río
Phone: (53 8) 27-8426

Jurásico

International cuisine
Villa Dos Hermanas.
Viñales. Pinar del Río
Phone: (53 8) 793223

Vera

International cuisine
Hotel Los Jazmines.
Viñales. Pinar del Río
Phone: (53 8) 93-6205

NIGHTLIFE
(VARADERO)

Acuabar Los Cocos
Pool bar
Hotel Arenas Doradas.
Cárdenas. Matanzas
Phone: (53 45) 66-8150

Gran Canal
Bar
Hotel Kawama.
Cárdenas. Matanzas
Phone: (53 45) 61-4416

Aguja
Piano bar
Hotel Las Morlas.
Cárdenas. Matanzas
Phone: (53 45) 66-7230

Grumete
Snack bar
Hotel Sol Sirenas-Coral.
Cárdenas. Matanzas
Phone: (53 45) 66-8070

Alisio
Lobby bar
Hotel Sol Sirenas-Coral.
Cárdenas. Matanzas
Phone: (53 45) 66-8070

Habana Café
Nightclub
Hotel Sol Sirenas-Coral.
Cárdenas. Matanzas
Phone: (53 45) 66-8070

Amelia
Bar
Hotel Club Amigo Varadero.
Cárdenas. Matanzas
Phone: (53 45) 66-8243

Havana Club
Disco
Calle 62 y 3ra.
Cárdenas. Matanzas
Phone: (53 45) 61-4555

Anaida
Pool bar
Hotel Brisas del Caribe.
Cárdenas. Matanzas
Phone: (53 45) 66-8030

Havana Club
Beach bar
Hotel Meliá Las Américas.
Cárdenas. Matanzas
Phone: (53 45) 66-7600

Aquabar
Pool bar
Hotel Meliá Las Américas.
Cárdenas. Matanzas
Phone: (53 45) 66-7600

Hicacos
Bar
Hotel Playa de Oro.
Cárdenas. Matanzas
Phone: (53 45) 66-8566

Arábica
Lobby bar
Hotel Brisas del Caribe.
Cárdenas. Matanzas
Phone: (53 45) 66-8030

Horizontes
Snack bar
Hotel Barceló Solymar Beach
Resort. Cárdenas. Matanzas
Phone: (53 45) 61-4499

Arcoiris
Bar
Hotel Club Puntarena.
Cárdenas. Matanzas
Phone: (53 45) 66-7125

Hoyo 19
Snack bar
Carretera Las Américas km. 8 ½,
Mansión Xanadu.
Cárdenas. Matanzas
Phone: (53 45) 66-7388

Areíto
Disco
Hotel Paradisus Varadero.
Cárdenas. Matanzas
Phone: (53 45) 66-8700

Isleta
Bar
Marina Dársena de Varadero.
Cárdenas. Matanzas
Phone: (53 45) 61-3730

Arrecife
Pool bar
Hotel Sol Sirenas-Coral.
Cárdenas. Matanzas
Phone: (53 45) 66-8070

Jardines Mediterráneo
Cabaret
Calle 1ra. y 54.
Cárdenas. Matanzas
Phone: (53 45) 61-2460

Arrecife
Pool bar
Hotel Tryp Península Varadero.
Cárdenas. Matanzas
Phone: (53 45) 66-8800

NIGHTLIFE
(VARADERO)

Karaoke 440
Nightclub
Camino del Mar e/ 14 y 15.
Cárdenas. Matanzas

Atabey
Snack bar
Hotel Turquesa.
Cárdenas. Matanzas
Phone: (53 45) 66-8471

Kiki´s
Snack bar
Calle 6 y Ave. 1ra.
Cárdenas. Matanzas

Bar Grill
Bar
Villas Punta Blanca.
Cárdenas. Matanzas
Phone: (53 45) 66-8050

La Bamba
Disco
Hotel Tuxpan.
Cárdenas. Matanzas
Phone: (53 45) 66-7560

Bar Karaoke
Nightclub
Autopista Sur km. 11 ½, Plaza
América. Cárdenas. Matanzas

La Barrica
Bar
Hotel Varadero Internacional.
Phone: (53 45) 66-7038

La Bomba
Disco
Hotel Playa de Oro. Cárdenas.
Phone: (53 45) 66-8566

Bar Karaoke
Karaoke
Hotel Arenas Blancas.
Cárdenas. Matanzas
Phone: (53 45) 61-4450

Bar Marino
Bar
Autopista Sur km. 11 ½, Plaza
América. Cárdenas. Matanzas
Phone: (53 45) 66-8181

La Boya
Pool bar
Hotel Barceló Marina Palace.
Cárdenas. Matanzas
Phone: (53 45) 66-9966

Bar Piscina
Bar
Calle 1ra. y 56, Parque Josone.
Cárdenas. Matanzas
Phone: (53 45) 66-7228

La Caleta
Beach bar
Hotel Brisas del Caribe.
Cárdenas. Matanzas
Phone: (53 45) 66-8030

Bar Piscina
Pool bar
Hotel Barceló Marina Palace.
Cárdenas. Matanzas
Phone: (53 45) 66-9966

La Carpa
Bar
Hotel Palma Real.
Cárdenas. Matanzas
Phone: (53 45) 61-4555

Bar Piscina
Pool bar
Hotel Breezes Varadero.
Cárdenas. Matanzas
Phone: (53 45) 66-7030

La Cascada
Lobby bar
Hotel Bella Costa.
Cárdenas. Matanzas
Phone: (53 45) 66-7210

Bar Piscina
Pool bar
Villas Punta Blanca.
Cárdenas. Matanzas
Phone: (53 45) 66-8050

La Colmena
Snack bar
Calle 1ra. e/ 25 y 26.
Cárdenas. Matanzas
Phone: (53 45) 66-7736

Bar Piscina
Pool bar
Hotel Meliá Las Américas.
Cárdenas. Matanzas
Phone: (53 45) 66-7600

La Flor de Asia
Bar
Calle 8 No. 228 e/ Camino del
Mar y Ave. Kawama.
Cárdenas. Matanzas

Bar Playa
Beach bar
Hotel Meliá Las Antillas.
Cárdenas. Matanzas
Phone: (53 45) 668470

NIGHTLIFE
(VARADERO)

La Gruta
Bar
Calle 1ra. y 56, Parque Josone.
Cárdenas. Matanzas
Phone: (53 45) 66-7228

Bar Playa
Beach bar
Hotel Taínos.
Cárdenas. Matanzas
Phone: (53 45) 66-8656

La Guarapera
Bar
Calle 1ra. y 56, Parque Josone.
Cárdenas. Matanzas
Phone: (53 45) 66-7228

Bar Playa
Beach bar
Hotel Las Morlas.
Cárdenas. Matanzas
Phone: (53 45) 66-7230

La Hacienda
Bar
Hotel Bella Costa.
Cárdenas. Matanzas
Phone: (53 45) 66-7210

Bar Playa
Bar
Hotel Cuatro Palmas.
Cárdenas. Matanzas
Phone: (53 45) 66-7040

La Oliva
Disco
Hotel Playa Alameda Varadero.
Cárdenas. Matanzas
Phone: (53 45) 66-8822

Bar Playa Fritada Criolla
Beach bar
Hotel Club Amigo Varadero.
Cárdenas. Matanzas
Phone: (53 45) 66-8243

La Orquídea
Lobby bar
Villa La Mar.
Cárdenas. Matanzas
Phone: (53 45) 61-3910

Bar Playa Saoco
Beach bar
Hotel Playa de Oro.
Cárdenas. Matanzas
Phone: (53 45) 66-8566

La Pachanga
Disco
Hotel Acuazul.
Cárdenas. Matanzas
Phone: (53 45) 66-7132

Bar Sala de Fiestas
Bar
Hotel Barceló Marina Palace.
Cárdenas. Matanzas
Phone: (53 45) 66-9966

La Palma
Lobby bar
Hotel Taínos.
Cárdenas. Matanzas
Phone: (53 45) 66-8656

Bar Teatro
Bar
Hotel Barceló Marina Palace.
Cárdenas. Matanzas
Phone: (53 45) 66-9966

La Patana
Nightclub
Vía Blanca. Cárdenas. Matanzas
Phone: (53 45) 61-9971

Baracoa
Pool bar
Hotel Meliá Varadero.
Cárdenas. Matanzas
Phone: (53 45) 66-7013

La Red
Disco
Villa La Mar.
Cárdenas. Matanzas
Phone: (53 45) 61-3910

Beach Club "Ranchón Bucanero"
Beach bar
Hotel Playa Alameda Varadero.
Cárdenas. Matanzas
Phone: (53 45) 66-8822

La Sangría
Snack bar
Calle 8 y Ave. 1ra.
Cárdenas. Matanzas
Phone: (53 45) 61-2025

Benny Bar
Bar
Camino del Mar e/ 12 y 13.
Cárdenas. Matanzas
Phone: (53 45) 61-3787

La Sirenita
Pool bar
Hotel Bella Costa.
Cárdenas. Matanzas
Phone: (53 45) 66-7210

NIGHTLIFE
(VARADERO)

Bergantín
Lobby bar
Hotel Sol Sirenas-Coral.
Cárdenas. Matanzas
Phone: (53 45) 66-8070

La Taberna
Snack bar
Camino del Mar e/ 13 y 14.
Cárdenas. Matanzas

Blue Star
Bar
Hotel Acuazul.
Cárdenas. Matanzas
Phone: (53 45) 66-7132

La Taberna
Bar
Hotel Breezes Varadero.
Cárdenas. Matanzas
Phone: (53 45) 66-7030

Bodegoncito
Snack bar
Ave. 1ra. y 40.
Cárdenas. Matanzas

La Tinaja
Lobby bar
Hotel Playa Alameda Varadero.
Cárdenas. Matanzas
Phone: (53 45) 66-8822

Bohío Mar
Bar
Camino del Mar e/ 10 y 11.
Cárdenas. Matanzas
Phone: (53 45) 61-2407

Laguna Azul
Snack bar
Hotel Playa Alameda Varadero.
Cárdenas. Matanzas
Phone: (53 45) 66-8822

Brisote
Pool bar
Hotel Sol Sirenas-Coral.
Cárdenas. Matanzas
Phone: (53 45) 66-8070

Las Américas
Lobby bar
Hotel Meliá Las Américas.
Cárdenas. Matanzas
Phone: (53 45) 66-7600

Buona Sera
Bar
Calle 1ra. y 11.
Cárdenas. Matanzas
Phone: (53 45) 61-2428

Las Brisas
Disco
Hotel Brisas del Caribe.
Cárdenas. Matanzas
Phone: (53 45) 66-8030

Calle 62
Snack bar
Ave. 1ra. y 22.
Cárdenas. Matanzas

Las Dunas
Snack bar
Hotel Barceló Solymar Beach
Resort. Cárdenas. Matanzas
Phone: (53 45) 61-4499

Camaguey
Bar
Hotel Club Amigo Varadero.
Cárdenas. Matanzas
Phone: (53 45) 66-8243

Las Olas
Snack bar
Hotel Cuatro Palmas.
Cárdenas. Matanzas
Phone: (53 45) 66-7040

Carabo
Beach bar
Hotel Paradisus Varadero.
Cárdenas. Matanzas
Phone: (53 45) 66-8700

Las Palmas
Piano bar
Hotel Meliá Varadero.
Cárdenas. Matanzas
Phone: (53 45) 66-7013

Caribe
Lobby bar
Hotel Brisas del Caribe.
Cárdenas. Matanzas
Phone: (53 45) 66-8030

Las Redes
Beach bar
Hotel Barceló Solymar Beach
Resort. Cárdenas. Matanzas
Phone: (53 45) 61-4499

Casa Blanca
Bar
Autopista Sur km. 8½, Mansión
Xanadú. Cárdenas. Matanzas
Phone: (53 45) 66-7388

NIGHTLIFE
(VARADERO)

Las Sirenas
Lobby bar
Hotel Las Morlas.
Cárdenas. Matanzas
Phone: (53 45) 66-7230

Casa de Al
Bar
Villas Punta Blanca.
Cárdenas. Matanzas
Phone: (53 45) 66-8050

Las Tejas
Lobby bar
Villas Punta Blanca.
Cárdenas. Matanzas
Phone: (53 45) 66-8050

Cascada
Bar
Hotel Club Puntarena.
Cárdenas. Matanzas
Phone: (53 45) 66-7125

Latino
Lobby bar
Hotel Varadero Internacional.
Cárdenas. Matanzas
Phone: (53 45) 66-7038

Cayo Libertad
Bar
Marina Dársena de Varadero.
Cárdenas. Matanzas
Phone: (53 45) 61-3730

Lecuona
Lobby bar
Hotel Tryp Península Varadero.
Cárdenas. Matanzas
Phone: (53 45) 66-8800

Chequere
Disco
Villa Cuba Resort.
Cárdenas. Matanzas
Phone: (53 45) 66-8280

Lobby Bar
Lobby bar
Hotel Club Tropical.
Cárdenas. Matanzas
Phone: (53 45) 61-3915

Club Hemingway
Lobby bar
Hotel Barceló Marina Palace.
Cárdenas. Matanzas
Phone: (53 45) 66-9966

Lobby Bar
Lobby bar
Hotel Tuxpan.
Cárdenas. Matanzas
Phone: (53 45) 66-7560

Coco Mar
Beach bar
Hotel Dos Mares.
Cárdenas. Matanzas
Phone: (53 45) 61-2702

Lobby Piano Bar
Bar
Hotel Meliá Las Antillas.
Cárdenas. Matanzas
Phone: (53 45) 668470

Continental
Cabaret
Hotel Varadero Internacional.
Cárdenas. Matanzas
Phone: (53 45) 66-7038

Los Corales
Snack bar
Hotel Los Delfines.
Cárdenas. Matanzas
Phone: (53 45) 66-7720

Coralia
Lobby bar
Hotel Cuatro Palmas.
Cárdenas. Matanzas
Phone: (53 45) 66-7040

Los Delfines
Bar
Hotel Barceló Solymar Beach
Resort. Cárdenas. Matanzas
Phone: (53 45) 61-4499

Cuba
Bar
Hotel Club Amigo Varadero.
Cárdenas. Matanzas
Phone: (53 45) 66-8243

Los Grumetes
Piano bar
Hotel Barceló Solymar Beach
Resort. Cárdenas. Matanzas
Phone: (53 45) 61-4499

Cubitas
Lobby bar
Hotel Sol Palmeras.
Cárdenas. Matanzas
Phone: (53 45) 66-7009

Los Pelícanos
Beach bar
Hotel Arenas Doradas.
Cárdenas. Matanzas
Phone: (53 45) 66-8150

NIGHTLIFE
(VARADERO)

Cueva del Pirata
Cabaret
Autopista Sur km. 11.
Cárdenas. Matanzas
Phone: (53 45) 66-7751

Mambo Club
Nightclub
Carretera Las Morlas km. 14.
Cárdenas. Matanzas
Phone: (53 45) 66-8565

Cusubi
Lobby bar
Hotel Paradisus Varadero.
Cárdenas. Matanzas
Phone: (53 45) 66-8700

Marengo
Beach bar
Hotel Playa Caleta.
Cárdenas. Matanzas
Phone: (53 45) 66-7120

Daikiri
Bar
Hotel Palma Real.
Cárdenas. Matanzas
Phone: (53 45) 61-4555

Martino´s
Bar
Hotel Breezes Varadero.
Cárdenas. Matanzas
Phone: (53 45) 66-7030

Disco Bar
Disco
Hotel Meliá Las Antillas.
Cárdenas. Matanzas
Phone: (53 45) 668470

Mediterráneo
Lobby bar
Hotel Sol Sirenas-Coral.
Cárdenas. Matanzas
Phone: (53 45) 66-8070

Disco Bar
Disco
Hotel Breezes Varadero.
Cárdenas. Matanzas
Phone: (53 45) 66-7030

Memories
Disco
Hotel Arenas Doradas.
Cárdenas. Matanzas
Phone: (53 45) 66-8150

Don Café
Bar
Hotel Taínos.
Cárdenas. Matanzas
Phone: (53 45) 66-8656

Mirador
Bar
Villa Cuba Resort.
Cárdenas. Matanzas
Phone: (53 45) 66-8280

Dos Mares
Snack bar
Hotel Dos Mares.
Cárdenas. Matanzas
Phone: (53 45) 61-2702

Mirador
Snack bar
Vía Blanca km. 18.
Cárdenas. Matanzas
Phone: (53 45) 61-1085

Duna
Bar
Hotel Breezes Varadero.
Cárdenas. Matanzas
Phone: (53 45) 66-7030

Mojito
Bar
Hotel Barlovento.
Cárdenas. Matanzas
Phone: (53 45) 66-7140

Eclipse
Disco
Hotel Sun Beach.
Cárdenas. Matanzas
Phone: (53 45) 66-7490

Náutico
Bar
Hotel Club Puntarena.
Cárdenas. Matanzas
Phone: (53 45) 66-7125

El Brocal
Beach bar
Villa Punta Blanca.
Cárdenas. Matanzas
Phone: (53 7) 66-8050

Noche Azul
Nightclub
Calle 60 e/ 2da. y 3ra.
Cárdenas. Matanzas
Phone: (53 45) 66-7415

El Cactus
Pool bar
Hotel Arenas Blancas.
Cárdenas. Matanzas
Phone: (53 45) 61-4450

NIGHTLIFE
(VARADERO)

Oasis
Bar
Hotel Oasis Tennis Centre.
Cárdenas. Matanzas
Phone: (53 45) 66-7380

El Camino
Bar
Camino del Mar y 11.
Cárdenas. Matanzas

Palacio de La Rumba
Disco
Ave. de Las Américas km. 4.
Cárdenas. Matanzas
Phone: (53 45) 66-8210

El Candil
Beach bar
Hotel Kawama.
Cárdenas. Matanzas
Phone: (53 45) 61-4416

Paso de Carretera Playazul
Snack bar
Vía Blanca km. 18.
Cárdenas. Matanzas
Phone: (53 45) 61-1085

El Caribeño
Bar
Villa Cuba Resort.
Cárdenas. Matanzas
Phone: (53 45) 66-8280

Piano Bar
Piano bar
Hotel Breezes Varadero.
Cárdenas. Matanzas
Phone: (53 45) 66-7030

El Centralito
Bar
Villas Punta Blanca.
Cárdenas. Matanzas
Phone: (53 45) 66-8050

Piano Bar Delirio
Piano bar
Hotel Brisas del Caribe.
Cárdenas. Matanzas
Phone: (53 45) 66-8030

El Chiringuito
Beach bar
Hotel Bella Costa.
Cárdenas. Matanzas
Phone: (53 45) 66-7210

Playa y Arenas
Snack bar
Hotel Arenas Blancas.
Cárdenas. Matanzas
Phone: (53 45) 61-4450

El Cocotero
Pool bar
Hotel Playa Caleta.
Cárdenas. Matanzas
Phone: (53 45) 66-7120

Plaza
Lobby bar
Hotel Barlovento.
Cárdenas. Matanzas
Phone: (53 45) 66-7140

El Colibrí
Snack bar
Hotel Tuxpan.
Cárdenas. Matanzas
Phone: (53 45) 66-7560

Plaza El Escambray
Lobby bar
Hotel Playa Caleta.
Cárdenas. Matanzas
Phone: (53 45) 66-7120

El Colonial
Lobby bar
Villa Cuba Resort.
Cárdenas. Matanzas
Phone: (53 45) 66-8280

Popeye's Bar
Bar
Hotel & Villas Tortuga.
Cárdenas. Matanzas
Phone: (53 45) 61-2622

El Coral
Bar
Hotel Playa de Oro.
Cárdenas. Matanzas
Phone: (53 45) 66-8566

Puesta de Sol
Bar
Villas Punta Blanca.
Cárdenas. Matanzas
Phone: (53 45) 66-8050

El Coral
Bar
Aparthotel Mar del Sur.
Cárdenas. Matanzas
Phone: (53 45) 61-2246

Ranchón
Bar
Aparthotel Mar del Sur.
Cárdenas. Matanzas
Phone: (53 45) 61-2246

NIGHTLIFE
(VARADERO)

El Coral
Snack bar
Villa La Mar.
Cárdenas. Matanzas
Phone: (53 45) 61-3910

Ranchón Bar
Bar
Ave. Playa e/ 52 y 53.
Cárdenas. Matanzas

El Delfín
Bar
Autopista Sur km. 12.
Cárdenas. Matanzas
Phone: (53 45) 66-8031

Ranchón Bar
Bar
Hotel Meliá Las Antillas.
Matanzas
Phone: (53 45) 668470

El Delfín
Beach bar
Hotel Tuxpan.
Cárdenas. Matanzas
Phone: (53 45) 66-7560

Ranchón Playa
Bar
Hotel Palma Real.
Cárdenas. Matanzas
Phone: (53 45) 61-4555

El Dorado
Snack bar
Hotel Kawama.
Cárdenas. Matanzas
Phone: (53 45) 61-4416

Ranchón Playa
Bar
Villa Cuba Resort.
Cárdenas. Matanzas
Phone: (53 45) 66-8280

El Emperador
Lobby bar
Hotel Los Delfines.
Cárdenas. Matanzas
Phone: (53 45) 66-7720

Rincón Cubano
Cabaret
Hotel Meliá Las Américas.
Cárdenas. Matanzas
Phone: (53 45) 66-7600

El Framboyán
Pool bar
Hotel Barlovento.
Cárdenas. Matanzas
Phone: (53 45) 66-7140

Rincón Latino
Bar
Hotel Bella Costa.
Cárdenas. Matanzas
Phone: (53 45) 66-7210

El Galeón
Lobby bar
Hotel Dos Mares.
Cárdenas. Matanzas
Phone: (53 45) 61-2702

Ron Coco
Snack bar
Hotel Sol Palmeras.
Cárdenas. Matanzas
Phone: (53 45) 66-7009

El Golfito
Bar
Calle 1ra. y 42.
Cárdenas. Matanzas

Ron Coco
Beach bar
Hotel Meliá Varadero.
Cárdenas. Matanzas
Phone: (53 45) 66-7013

El Kastillito
Nightclub
Ave. Playa e/ 48 y 49.
Cárdenas. Matanzas
Phone: (53 45) 61-3888

Santiago
Cabaret
Hotel Meliá Varadero.
Cárdenas. Matanzas
Phone: (53 45) 66-7013

El Mirador
Bar
Hotel Bella Costa.
Cárdenas. Matanzas
Phone: (53 45) 66-7210

Saoco
Snack bar
Hotel Tryp Península Varadero.
Cárdenas. Matanzas
Phone: (53 45) 66-8800

El Mojito
Pool bar
Hotel Sol Palmeras.
Cárdenas. Matanzas
Phone: (53 45) 66-7009

NIGHTLIFE
(VARADERO)

Saoko
Bar
Hotel Palma Real.
Cárdenas. Matanzas
Phone: (53 45) 61-4555

El Mojito
Bar
Hotel Palma Real.
Cárdenas. Matanzas
Phone: (53 45) 61-4555

Siboney
Bar
Hotel Turquesa.
Cárdenas. Matanzas
Phone: (53 45) 66-8471

El Mojito
Lobby bar
Hotel Turquesa.
Cárdenas. Matanzas
Phone: (53 45) 66-8471

Sol Cubano
Beach bar
Hotel Sol Palmeras.
Cárdenas. Matanzas
Phone: (53 45) 66-7009

El Náutico
Bar
Aparthotel Mar del Sur.
Cárdenas. Matanzas
Phone: (53 45) 61-2246

Solymar
Lobby bar
Hotel Barceló Solymar Beach
Resort. Cárdenas. Matanzas
Phone: (53 45) 61-4499

El Patio
Lobby bar
Hotel Arenas Doradas.
Cárdenas. Matanzas
Phone: (53 45) 66-8150

Splash
Disco
Villa Punta Blanca.
Cárdenas. Matanzas
Phone: (53 45) 66-7090

El Peñón
Bar
Hotel Club Amigo Varadero.
Cárdenas. Matanzas
Phone: (53 45) 66-8243

Taíno
Bar
Hotel Brisas del Caribe.
Cárdenas. Matanzas
Phone: (53 45) 66-8030

El Picante
Bar
Hotel Varadero Internacional.
Cárdenas. Matanzas
Phone: (53 45) 66-7038

Tea Corner
Lobby bar
Hotel Sol Sirenas-Coral.
Cárdenas. Matanzas
Phone: (53 45) 66-8070

El Pony
Lobby bar
Hotel Herradura.
Cárdenas. Matanzas
Phone: (53 45) 61-3703

Teclado
Lobby bar
Hotel Arenas Blancas.
Cárdenas. Matanzas
Phone: (53 45) 61-4450

El Ranchón
Pool bar
Hotel Taínos.
Cárdenas. Matanzas
Phone: (53 45) 66-8656

Tenerife
Karaoke
Hotel Meliá Varadero.
Cárdenas. Matanzas
Phone: (53 45) 66-7013

El Ranchoncito
Bar
Calle 1ra. y 40.
Cárdenas. Matanzas

Tennis Bar
Bar
Hotel Breezes Varadero.
Cárdenas. Matanzas
Phone: (53 45) 66-7030

El Rincón
Bar
Camino del Mar e/ 11 y 12.
Cárdenas. Matanzas

Toa
Pool bar
Hotel Paradisus Varadero.
Cárdenas. Matanzas
Phone: (53 45) 66-8700

NIGHTLIFE
(VARADERO)

El Taíno
Beach bar
Hotel Turquesa.
Cárdenas. Matanzas
Phone: (53 45) 66-8471

Tocororo
Bar
Hotel Palma Real.
Cárdenas. Matanzas
Phone: (53 45) 61-4555

El Trópico
Bar
Aparthotel Mar del Sur.
Cárdenas. Matanzas
Phone: (53 45) 61-2246

Tramontana
Beach bar
Hotel Sol Sirenas-Coral.
Cárdenas. Matanzas
Phone: (53 45) 66-7240

Espiral
Bar
Hotel Club Puntarena.
Cárdenas. Matanzas
Phone: (53 45) 66-7125

Trinidad
Bar
Hotel Club Amigo Varadero.
Cárdenas. Matanzas
Phone: (53 45) 66-8243

Esplanada Teatro
Bar
Hotel Playa Alameda Varadero.
Cárdenas. Matanzas
Phone: (53 45) 66-8822

Tropi Fruti
Bar
Hotel Bella Costa.
Cárdenas. Matanzas
Phone: (53 45) 66-7210

Extasis
Bar
Villa Cuba Resort.
Cárdenas. Matanzas
Phone: (53 45) 66-8280

Tropi Gala
Cabaret
Hotel Tuxpan. Cárdenas.
Phone: (53 45) 66-7560

FM-13
Snack bar
Calle 1ra. y 13.
Cárdenas. Matanzas

Tropical
Beach bar
Hotel Club Puntarena. Cárdenas
Phone: (53 45) 66-7125

Tropicuba
Nightclub
Hotel Sol Palmeras. Cárdenas.
Phone: (53 45) 66-7009

Varadero
Bar
Hotel Brisas del Caribe.
Cárdenas. Matanzas
Phone: (53 45) 66-8030

Fun Pub
Nightclub
Hotel Sol Palmeras. Cárdenas.
Phone: (53 45) 66-7009

FM-23
Snack bar
Ave. 1ra. y 23.
Cárdenas. Matanzas

Turquesa
Beach bar
Hotel Sol Sirenas-Coral.
Cárdenas. Matanzas
Phone: (53 45) 66-8070

FM-27
Snack bar
Ave. 1ra. y 27.
Cárdenas. Matanzas

Turquino
Bar
Hotel Sol Palmeras.
Cárdenas. Matanzas
Phone: (53 45) 66-7009

Fortuna
Lobby bar
Hotel Kawama. Cárdenas.
Phone: (53 45) 61-4416

Varadero
Cabaret
Vía Blanca km. 31 y Carretera a
Cárdenas. Cárdenas. Matanzas
Phone: (53 45) 66-7130

Fruti Tuxpan
Bar
Hotel Tuxpan. Cárdenas.
Phone: (53 45) 66-7560

Veraclub
Beach bar
Villas Punta Blanca. Cárdenas.
Phone: (53 45) 66-8050

NIGHTLIFE
(HAVANA COLONIAL)

Ambos Mundos

Bar

Hotel Ambos Mundos.
La Habana Vieja. La Habana
Phone: (53 7) 860-9530

La Dichosa

Bar

Calle Obispo esq. a Compostela.
La Habana Vieja. La Habana
Phone: (53 7) 861-5292

Anacaona

Bar

Hotel Saratoga.
La Habana Vieja. La Habana
Phone: (53 7) 868-1000

La Lluvia de Oro

Bar

Calle Obispo esq. a Habana.
La Habana Vieja. La Habana
Phone: (53 7) 862-9870

Bar Café Maragato

Bar

Hotel Florida.
La Habana Vieja. La Habana
Phone: (53 7) 862-4127

La Marina

Lobby bar

Hotel Armadores de Santander.
La Habana Vieja. La Habana
Phone: (53 7) 862-8000

Bar Mezanine

Bar

Hotel Saratoga.
La Habana Vieja. La Habana
Phone: (53 7) 868-1000

La Mina

Bar

Calle Obispo No. 106 esq. a
Oficios. La Habana Vieja.
Phone: (53 7) 862-0216

Bar Monserrate

Bar

Calle Monserrate esq. a Obrapía.
La Habana Vieja. La Habana
Phone: (53 7) 860-9751

La Sevillana

Lobby bar

Hotel Inglaterra. La Habana
Vieja. La Habana
Phone: (53 7) 860-8594

Bosque de Boloña

Bar

Calle Obispo No. 464 e/ Villegas
y Aguacate. La Habana Vieja.
Phone: (53 7) 866-4139

La Terraza

Bar

Hotel Inglaterra. La Habana
Vieja. La Habana
Phone: (53 7) 860-8594

Café O´Reilly

Bar

Calle O´Reilly e/ San Ignacio y
Cuba. La Habana Vieja.
La Habana

Lobby Bar

Lobby bar

Hotel Palacio San Miguel.
La Habana Vieja. La Habana
Phone: (53 7) 862-7656

Café París

Bar

Calle San Ignacio esq. a Obispo.
La Habana Vieja. La Habana

Lobby Bar

Lobby bar

Hotel Caribbean. Centro
Habana. La Habana
Phone: (53 7) 860-8233

Chico O´Farrill

Snack bar

Hotel Palacio O´Farrill.
La Habana Vieja. La Habana
Phone: (53 7) 860-5080

Lobby Bar

Lobby bar

Hotel Los Frailes.
La Habana Vieja. La Habana
Phone: (53 7) 862-9383

Disco Karaoke

Disco

Hotel Plaza.
La Habana Vieja. La Habana
Phone: (53 7) 860-8583

Los Marinos

Snack bar

Ave. del Puerto e/ Justiz y
Obrapía. La Habana Vieja.
La Habana
Phone: (53 7) 33-8808

Dos Hermanos

Bar

Ave. del Puerto esq. a Santa
Clara. La Habana Vieja.
Phone: (53 7) 861-3514

NIGHTLIFE
(HAVANA COLONIAL)

Lounge Alameda
Bar
Hotel Parque Central.
La Habana Vieja. La Habana
Phone: (53 7) 860-6627

El Floridita
Bar
Calle Obispo No. 557.
La Habana Vieja. La Habana
Phone: (53 7) 867-1300

Mirador Saratoga
Snack bar
Hotel Saratoga.
La Habana Vieja. La Habana
Phone: (53 7) 868-1000

El Louvre
Snack bar
Hotel Inglaterra. La Habana
Vieja. La Habana
Phone: (53 7) 860-8594

Nostalgia
Bar
Hostal Valencia. La Habana
Vieja. La Habana
Phone: (53 7) 867-1037

El Patio
Bar
Calle San Ignacio No. 54,
Plaza de la Catedral.
La Habana Vieja. La Habana
Phone: (53 7) 867-1035

El Pórtico
Lobby bar
Hotel Parque Central.
La Habana Vieja. La Habana
Phone: (53 7) 860-6627

Santovenia
Lobby bar
Hotel Santa Isabel.
La Habana Vieja. La Habana
Phone: (53 7) 860-8201

Fausto
Bar
Hotel Plaza.
La Habana Vieja. La Habana
Phone: (53 7) 860-8583

Solarium
Bar
Hotel Plaza.
La Habana Vieja. La Habana
Phone: (53 7) 860-8583

Florida
Lobby bar
Hotel Florida.
La Habana Vieja. La Habana
Phone: (53 7) 862-4127

Terraza Mirador
Snack bar
Hotel Palacio San Miguel.
La Habana Vieja. La Habana
Phone: (53 7) 862-7656

Vitral
Lobby bar
Hotel Plaza.
La Habana Vieja. La Habana
Phone: (53 7) 860-8583

La Bodeguita del Medio
Bar
Calle Empedrado No. 206.
La Habana Vieja. La Habana
Phone: (53 7) 867-1374

Nuevo Mundo
Bar
Hotel Parque Central.
La Habana Vieja. La Habana
Phone: (53 7) 860-6627

Fundación Ron Havana Club
Bar
Calle San Pedro No. 262 e/
Sol y Muralla. La Habana Vieja.
Phone: (53 7) 861-1900

NIGHTLIFE
(HAVANA CITY)

70`s Café
Disco
Hotel Deauville.
Centro Habana. La Habana
Phone: (53 7) 866-8812

La Cecilia
Cabaret
5ta. Ave. e/ 110 y 112,
Miramar. Playa. La Habana
Phone: (53 7) 204-1562

Aire Mar
Bar
Hotel Nacional de Cuba. Plaza
de la Revolución. La Habana
Phone: (53 7) 836-3564

La Conga
Bar
Hotel Tropicoco.
La Habana del Este. La Habana
Phone: (53 7) 797-1371

Arrecifes
Snack bar
Hotel Mariposa.
La Lisa. La Habana
Phone: (53 7) 204-9137

La Fuente
Bar
5ta. Ave. e/ 110 y 112,
Miramar. Playa. La Habana
Phone: (53 7) 204-1562

Arrecifes
Snack bar
Hotel Chateau Miramar.
Playa. La Habana
Phone: (53 7) 204-1957

La Maison
Bar
Calle 16 e/ 7ma. y 9na.,
Miramar. Playa. La Habana
Phone: (53 7) 204-1543

Atardecer
Bar
Hotel Lincoln. Centro Habana.
Phone: (53 7) 862-8061

La Pérgola
Disco
Hotel Comodoro.
Playa. La Habana
Phone: (53 7) 204-5551

Atlántico
Cabaret
Hotel Atlántico.
La Habana del Este.
Phone: (53 7) 797-1085

La Zorra y el Cuervo Jazz Club
Nightclub
Calle 23 e/ N y O, Vedado. Plaza
de la Revolución. La Habana
Phone: (53 7) 833-2402

Atlántico
Snack bar
Aparthotel Atlántico.
La Habana del Este.
Phone: (53 7) 797-1494

Las Bulerías
Nightclub
Calle L e/ 23 y 25, Vedado. Plaza
de la Revolución. La Habana
Phone: (53 7) 832-3283

Atlántico
Pool bar
Aparthotel Atlántico.
La Habana del Este.
Phone: (53 7) 797-1494

Las Terrazas
Bar
Aparthotel Las Terrazas.
La Habana del Este.
Phone: (53 7) 797-1315

Bar Arenas
Bar
Villa Armonía Tarará. La
Habana del Este. La Habana
Phone: (53 7) 796-1616

Las Terrazas
Pool bar
Aparthotel Las Terrazas.
La Habana del Este.
Phone: (53 7) 797-1315

Bar Azul
Bar
Hotel Capri. Plaza de la
Revolución. La Habana
Phone: (53 7) 833-3747

Las Vistas
Pool bar
Villas Mirador del Mar.
La Habana del Este.
Phone: (53 7) 797-1362

Bar Longina
Bar
Calle 20 No. 3308 esq. a 35,
Miramar. Playa. La Habana
Phone: (53 7) 204-0447

NIGHTLIFE
(HAVANA CITY)

Lido
Lobby bar
Hotel Lido. Centro Habana.
La Habana
Phone: (53 7) 862-0653

Bar Piscina
Bar
Hotel Tropicoco.
La Habana del Este. La Habana
Phone: (53 7) 797-1371

Lirio
Bar
Hotel Kohly. Playa. La Habana
Phone: (53 7) 204-0240

Bar piscina
Pool bar
Hotel Bello Caribe.
Playa. La Habana
Phone: (53 7) 273-9906

Lobby Bar
Bar
Hotel Comodoro. Playa.
Phone: (53 7) 204-5551

Bar piscina
Pool bar
Hotel El Viejo y El Mar. Playa.
Phone: (53 7) 204-6820

Lobby Bar
Bar
Hotel Kohly. Playa. La Habana
Phone: (53 7) 204-0240

Bar piscina
Pool bar
Hotel La Pradera. Playa.
Phone: (53 7) 273-7467

Lobby Bar
Bar
Hotel Occidental Miramar.
Playa. La Habana
Phone: (53 7) 204-3584

Bar Playa
Beach bar
Hotel Comodoro.
Playa. La Habana
Phone: (53 7) 204-5551

Lobby Bar
Lobby bar
Hotel Bello Caribe.
Playa. La Habana
Phone: (53 7) 273-9906

Bodegón de los Vinos
Snack bar
Parque Histórico Militar
Morro-Cabaña.
La Habana del Este. La Habana
Phone: (53 7) 866-6475

Lobby Bar
Lobby bar
Hotel Copacabana.
Playa. La Habana
Phone: (53 7) 204-1037

Boleros
Bar
Hotel Atlántico.
La Habana del Este. La Habana
Phone: (53 7) 797-1085

Los Delfines
Snack bar
Hotel Comodoro.
Playa. La Habana
Phone: (53 7) 204-5551

Café Cantante "Mi Habana"
Nightclub
Teatro Nacional de Cuba,
Calle Paseo y 39. Plaza de la
Revolución. La Habana
Phone: (53 7) 878-4273

Los Marinos
Snack bar
Villas Mirador del Mar.
La Habana del Este. La Habana
Phone: (53 7) 797-1362

Café Rodney
Bar
Calle 72 e/ 41 y 45.
Marianao. La Habana
Phone: (53 7) 267-1717

Los Nísperos
Snack bar
Hotel Bello Caribe.
Playa. La Habana
Phone: (53 7) 273-9906

Caipirinha
Snack bar
Hotel Copacabana.
Playa. La Habana
Phone: (53 7) 204-1037

Los Perritos
Snack bar
Hotel Colina. Plaza de la
Revolución. La Habana
Phone: (53 7) 836-4071

Capri
Pool bar
Hotel Capri. Plaza de la
Revolución. La Habana
Phone: (53 7) 833-3747

NIGHTLIFE
(HAVANA CITY)

Los Tres Monitos
Bar
Hotel Lincoln.
Centro Habana. La Habana
Phone: (53 7) 862-8061

Capri
Lobby bar
Hotel Capri. Plaza de la
Revolución. La Habana
Phone: (53 7) 833-3747

Macumba Habana
Nightclub
Calle 222 e/ 37 y Autopista,
Reparto La Coronela.
La Lisa. La Habana
Phone: (53 7) 273-0568

Capri
Bar
Hotel Capri. Plaza de la
Revolución. La Habana
Phone: (53 7) 833-3747

Marea Baja
Cabaret
Hotel Mégano.
La Habana del Este.
Phone: (53 7) 797-1610

Casa de la Música
Nightclub
Calle 20 No. 3308 esq. a 35,
Miramar. Playa. La Habana
Phone: (53 7) 202-6147

Mégano
Snack bar
Hotel Mégano.
La Habana del Este.
Phone: (53 7) 797-1610

Casa de la Música
Nightclub
Calle Galiano e/ Neptuno y
Concordia. Centro Habana.
Phone: (53 7) 862-4165

Mi Rinconcito
Bar
Ave. de las Terrazas y Ave. 5ª.
Sta. María del Mar.
La Habana del Este.
Phone: (53 7) 797-1361

Chan Chan
Nightclub
Marina Hemingway.
Playa. La Habana
Phone: (53 7) 204-4698

Mirador
Bar
Villas Mirador del Mar.
La Habana del Este.
Phone: (53 7) 797-1362

Chévere
Snack bar
Calle 49-C y 28-A, Reparto
Kohly. Playa. La Habana
Phone: (53 7) 204-4990

Mirador de Bellomonte
Nightclub
Vía Blanca, Alturas de Marbella.
La Habana del Este.
Phone: (53 7) 796-3431

Club Arenal
Lobby bar
Hotel Blau Club Arenal.
La Habana del Este.
Phone: (53 7) 797-1272

Mom Petit Chateau
Lobby bar
Hotel Mariposa.
La Lisa. La Habana
Phone: (53 7) 204-9137

Club Hoyo 19
Bar
Club de Golf Habana, Carretera
de Vento km. 8, Capdevila.
Boyeros. La Habana
Phone: (53 7) 649-8918

Mon Petit Chateau
Lobby bar
Hotel Chateau Miramar.
Playa. La Habana
Phone: (53 7) 204-1957

Club Imágenes
Nightclub
Calle Calzada y C, Vedado.
Plaza de la Revolución.
La Habana
Phone: (53 7) 833-3606

Neptuno
Lobby bar
Hotel Neptuno-Tritón. Playa
Phone: (53 7) 204-1606

Cocktail Blue
Piano bar
Hotel Meliá Cohiba.
Plaza de la Revolución.
Phone: (53 7) 833-3636

Neptuno
Snack bar
Marina Tarará.
La Habana del Este.
Phone: (53 7) 796-0240

NIGHTLIFE
(HAVANA CITY)

Colina
Lobby bar
Hotel Colina. Plaza de la
Revolución. La Habana
Phone: (53 7) 836-4071

Obenque
Snack bar
Marina Tarará.
La Habana del Este.
Phone: (53 7) 796-0240

Copa Room
Cabaret
Hotel Habana Riviera.
Plaza de la Revolución.
Phone: (53 7) 836-4051

Opus
Bar
Calle Calzada y D, Vedado,
Teatro "Amadeo Roldán".
Plaza de la Revolución.
Phone: (53 7) 832-4521

Coral
Lobby bar
Aparthotel Montehabana.
Playa. La Habana
Phone: (53 7) 206-9595

Papa´s
Disco
Ave. 7ª y 26 Playa.
Playa. La Habana
Phone: (53 7) 209-7920

Debba
Lobby bar
Hotel Acuario , Marina
Hemingway. Playa. La Habana
Phone: (53 7) 204-7628

Parisién
Cabaret
Hotel Nacional de Cuba.
Plaza de la Revolución.
Phone: (53 7) 836-3564

Delirio Habanero
Piano bar
Teatro Nacional de Cuba, Paseo
y 39. Plaza de la Revolución.
Phone: (53 7) 878-4275

Piano bar
Piano bar
Hotel Acuario , Marina
Hemingway. Playa. La Habana
Phone: (53 7) 204-7628

Discobar
Disco
Hotel Panamericano Resort.
La Habana del Este.
Phone: (53 7) 766-1010

Piano Mar
Bar
Hotel Habana Riviera.
Plaza de la Revolución.
Phone: (53 7) 836-4051

El Arpón
Bar
Villas Mirador del Mar.
La Habana del Este.
Phone: (53 7) 797-1362

Pico Blanco
Rincón del Feeling
Nightclub
Hotel St. John´s. Plaza de la
Revolución. La Habana
Phone: (53 7) 833-3740

El Carey
Snack bar
Villa Bacuranao.
La Habana del Este.
Phone: (53 7) 65-7645

Piel Canela
Cabaret
Calle 7ma. y 16,
Miramar. Playa. La Habana
Phone: (53 7) 204-1543

El Cobijo Real
VIP bar
Hotel Meliá Cohiba. Plaza de
la Revolución. La Habana
Phone: (53 7) 833-3636

Piscina Bar Grill
Bar
Hotel Tryp Habana Libre. Plaza
de la Revolución. La Habana
Phone: (53 7) 834-6100

El Cobo
Pool bar
Hotel Meliá Habana.
Playa. La Habana
Phone: (53 7) 204-8500

Piscina Snack Bar
Pool bar
Hotel Nacional de Cuba. Plaza
de la Revolución. La Habana
Phone: (53 7) 836-3564

El Cortijo
Nightclub
Hotel Vedado. Plaza de la
Revolución. La Habana
Phone: (53 7) 836-4072

NIGHTLIFE
(HAVANA CITY)

El Mirador

Bar

Hotel Deauville.
Centro Habana. La Habana
Phone: (53 7) 866-8812

Rincón Cubano

Lobby bar

Hotel Comodoro.
Playa. La Habana
Phone: (53 7) 204-5551

El Náutico

Pool bar

Villas Mirador del Mar.
La Habana del Este.
Phone: (53 7) 797-1362

Rincón del Bolero

Nightclub

Calle 7ma. y 26,
Miramar. Playa. La Habana
Phone: (53 7) 204-2353

El Patio

Bar

Hotel Habana Libre Tryp. Plaza
de la Revolución. La Habana
Phone: (53 7) 834-6100

Robaina

Cigar-tasting hall

Hotel Meliá Habana.
Playa. La Habana
Phone: (53 7) 204-8500

El Polvorín

Snack bar

Ave. Monumental, La Cabaña.
La Habana del Este. La Habana
Phone: (53 7) 863-8295

Saint John´s

Snack bar

Hotel Saint John´s. Plaza de
la Revolución. La Habana
Phone: (53 7) 833-3740

El Relicario

Cigar-tasting hall

Hotel Meliá Cohiba. Plaza de
la Revolución. La Habana
Phone: (53 7) 833-3636

Salón Bohemio

Disco

Hotel Neptuno-Tritón.
Playa. La Habana
Phone: (53 7) 204-1606

El Tucán

Nightclub

Villa Bacuranao.
La Habana del Este.
Phone: (53 7) 765-7645

Salón Rojo

Cabaret

Hotel Capri. Plaza de la
Revolución. La Habana
Phone: (53 7) 833-3747

El Turquino

Cabaret

Hotel Habana Libre Tryp.
Plaza de la Revolución.
Phone: (53 7) 834-6100

Salón "Benny Moré"

Nightclub

Jardines de la Cervecería
"La Tropical". Marianao.
Phone: (53 7) 206-1282

Expresso Bar

Lobby bar

Hotel Meliá Cohiba. Plaza de
la Revolución. La Habana
Phone: (53 7) 833-3636

Salón Verde

Bar

Club de Golf Habana, Carretera
de Vento km. 8, Capdevila.
Boyeros. La Habana
Phone: (53 7) 33-8818

Galería

Bar

Hotel Nacional de Cuba. Plaza
de la Revolución. La Habana
Phone: (53 7) 836-3564

Salsa Caliente

Nightclub

Hotel Mariposa.
La Lisa. La Habana
Phone: (53 7) 204-9137

Gato Tuerto Café Concert

Nightclub

Calle O e/ 17 y 19, Vedado.
Plaza de la Revolución.
Phone: (53 7) 838-2696

Saoco Bar

Bar

Hotel Tropicoco.
La Habana del Este. La Habana
Phone: (53 7) 797-1371

Gaviota

Bar

Hotel Kohly. Playa. La Habana
Phone: (53 7) 204-0240

NIGHTLIFE
(HAVANA CITY)

Siboney
Piano bar
Hotel Habana Libre Tryp.
Plaza de la Revolución.
Phone: (53 7) 834-6100

Gran Añejo
Lobby bar
Hotel Meliá Cohiba.
Plaza de la Revolución
Phone: (53 7) 833-3636

Snack bar
Snack bar
Hotel La Pradera. Playa.
La Habana
Phone: (53 7) 273-7467

Guanabo Club
Bar
Calle 468 e/ 13 y 15, Playa
Guanabo. La Habana del Este.
Phone: (53 7) 796-3210

Snack Bar Piscina
Snack bar
Hotel Habana Riviera.
Plaza de la Revolución.
Phone: (53 7) 836-4051

Guanabo Club
Cabaret
Calle 468 e/ 13 y 15, Playa
Guanabo. La Habana del Este.
Phone: (53 7) 796-3210

Tritón
Lobby bar
Hotel Neptuno-Tritón. Playa.
Phone: (53 7) 204-1606

Guarapera
Bar
Hotel Copacabana.
Playa. La Habana
Phone: (53 7) 204-1037

Tropicana
Cabaret
Calle 72 e/ 41 y 45.
Marianao. La Habana
Phone: (53 7) 267-1717

Habana Café
Nightclub
Hotel Meliá Cohiba.
Plaza de la Revolución.
Phone: (53 7) 833-3636

Vedado
VIP bar
Hotel Meliá Habana.
Playa. La Habana
Phone: (53 7) 204-8500

Habanos
Bar
Hotel Nacional de Cuba.
Plaza de la Revolución.
Phone: (53 7) 836-3564

Vedado
Lobby bar
Hotel Vedado. Plaza de la
Revolución. La Habana
Phone: (53 7) 836-4072

Havana Club
Disco
Calle 1ra. y 86,
Miramar. Playa. La Habana
Phone: (53 7) 204-2902

Victoria
Lobby bar
Hotel Victoria. Plaza de
la Revolución. La Habana
Phone: (53 7) 833-3510

Irakere Jazz Club
Nightclub
Calle A e/ 3ra. y 5ta
Miramar. Playa. La Habana

Victoria
Pool bar
Hotel Victoria. Plaza de la
Revolución. La Habana
Phone: (53 7) 833-3510

Jardín de la Terraza
Nightclub
Hotel Lincoln.
Centro Habana. La Habana
Phone: (53 7) 862-8061

Villa Paraíso
Snack bar
Hotel Acuario , Marina
Hemingway. Playa. La Habana
Phone: (53 7) 204-7628

Jazz Café
Nightclub
Calle Paseo y 3ra., Galerías
Paseo. Plaza de la Revolución.
La Habana
Phone: (53 7) 838-3556

Vista al Golfo
Bar
Hotel Nacional de Cuba.
Plaza de la Revolución.
Phone: (53 7) 836-3564

NIGHTLIFE
(SANTIAGO DE CUBA)

Alameda
Pool bar
Hotel Meliá Santiago de Cuba.
Santiago de Cuba
Phone: (53 22) 687070

La Conga
Bar
Hotel Bucanero.
Santiago de Cuba
Phone: (53 22) 68-6363

Anacaona
Bar
Motel Rancho Club.
Santiago de Cuba
Phone: (53 22) 63-3202

La Pachanga
Disco
Hotel Carisol-Los Corales.
Santiago de Cuba
Phone: (53 22) 35-6150

Bar Daiquirí
Lobby bar
Hotel Meliá Santiago de Cuba.
Santiago de Cuba
Phone: (53 22) 687070

La Pérgola
Bar
Hotel El Saltón. Tercer Frente.
Santiago de Cuba
Phone: (53 225) 6492

Bello Bar
Nightclub
Hotel Meliá Santiago de Cuba.
Santiago de Cuba
Phone: (53 22) 687070

La Salsa
Pool bar
Hotel Carisol-Los Corales.
Santiago de Cuba
Phone: (53 22) 35-6150

Café Cantante Niágara
Piano bar
Ave. de los Desfiles, Teatro
Heredia. Santiago de Cuba

La Taberna del Ron
Bar
Calle Carnicería e/ San Basilio
y Santa Lucía. Santiago de Cuba

Calypso
Lobby bar
Hotel Carisol-Los Corales.
Santiago de Cuba
Phone: (53 22) 35-6150

Las Acacias
Bar
Villa Santiago de Cuba.
Santiago de Cuba
Phone: (53 22) 64 1368

Centro Nocturno
Nightclub
-Hotel Costa Morena.
Santiago de Cuba
Phone: (53 22) 635- 6126

Club 300
Nightclub
Calle Aguilera No. 302 e/ San
Pedro y San Félix.
Santiago de Cuba
Phone: (53 22) 65-3532

Lobby Bar
Lobby bar
Hotel San Juan.
Santiago de Cuba
Phone: (53 22) 68-7200

Club Nocturno
Nightclub
Hotel Versalles.
Santiago de Cuba
Phone: (53 22) 691-016

Lobby Bar
Lobby bar
Hotel Versalles.
Santiago de Cuba
Phone: (53 22) 691-016

Club Tropical
Disco
Autopista Nacional km. 1 ½.
Santiago de Cuba
Phone: (53 22) 64-3036

Marino
Bar
Hotel Costa Morena.
Santiago de Cuba
Phone: (53 22) 635- 6126

Don Emilio
Bar
Villa Santiago de Cuba.
Santiago de Cuba
Phone: (53 22) 64 1368

Las Américas
Bar
Hotel Las Américas.
Santiago de Cuba
Phone: (53 22) 64-2011

NIGHTLIFE
(SANTIAGO DE CUBA)

Merengue

Pool bar

Hotel Carisol-Los Corales.

Santiago de Cuba

Phone: (53 22) 35-6150

El Caneysito

Snack bar

Motel Rancho Club.

Santiago de Cuba

Phone: (53 22) 63-3202

Mirador

Bar

Hotel El Saltón. Tercer Frente.

Santiago de Cuba

Phone: (53 225) 6492

El Copero

Lobby bar

Hotel Balcón del Caribe.

Santiago de Cuba

Phone: (53 22) 691-506

Patio Bar Paticruzao

Bar

Autopista Nacional km. 1 ½.

Santiago de Cuba

Phone: (53 22) 68-7020

El Pino

Snack bar

Hotel Versalles.

Santiago de Cuba

Phone: (53 22) 691-016

El Quijote

Nightclub

Hotel San Juan.

Santiago de Cuba

Phone: (53 22) 68-7200

Ranchón

Bar

Hotel El Saltón. Tercer Frente.

Santiago de Cuba

Phone: (53 225) 6492

Gran Piedra

Bar

Hotel Gran Piedra.

Santiago de Cuba

Phone: (53 22) 686147

Roof Garden

Bar

Hotel Casa Granda.

Santiago de Cuba

Phone: (53 22) 68-6600

La Bamba

Beach bar

Hotel Carisol-Los Corales.

Santiago de Cuba

Phone: (53 22) 35-6150

San Pedro del Mar

Cabaret

Carretera del Morro km. 7½.

Santiago de Cuba

Phone: (53 22) 69-1287

Tango

Lobby bar

Hotel Carisol-Los Corales.

Santiago de Cuba

Phone: (53 22) 35-6150

La Cascada

Bar

Hotel El Saltón. Tercer Frente.

Santiago de Cuba

Phone: (53 225) 6492

Tropicana Santiago

Cabaret

Autopista Nacional km. 1 ½.

Santiago de Cuba

Phone: (53 22) 64-3036

Rancho Club

Cabaret

Motel Rancho Club.

Santiago de Cuba

Phone: (53 22) 63-3202

La Caleta

Beach bar

Hotel Bucanero.

Santiago de Cuba

Phone: (53 22) 68-6363

NIGHTLIFE
(HOLGUÍN)

1492
Lobby bar
Hotel Sol Río de Luna y Mares.
Rafael Freyre. Holguín
Phone: (53 24) 3-0030

La Dolce Vita
Disco
Hotel Guardalavaca.
Banes. Holguín
Phone: (53 24) 3-0218

Acuabar
Bar
Hotel Guardalavaca.
Banes. Holguín
Phone: (53 24) 3-0218

La Fuente
Lobby bar
Hotel Blau Costa Verde.
Rafael Freyre. Holguín
Phone: (53 24) 3-0510

Antílope
Bar
Villa Cayo Saetía.
Mayarí. Holguín
Phone: (53 24) 96900

La Nao
Pool bar
Hotel Sol Río de Luna y Mares.
Rafael Freyre. Holguín
Phone: (53 24) 3-0030

Aquabar
Pool bar
Hotel Playa Costa Verde.
Rafael Freyre. Holguín
Phone: (53 24) 3-0520

La Niña
Lobby bar
Hotel Atlántico-Guardalavaca.
Banes. Holguín
Phone: (53 24) 3-0195

Arenas Nuevas
Bar
Villa Don Lino.
Rafael Freyre. Holguín
Phone: (53 24) 3-0259

La Pinta
Pool bar
Hotel Atlántico-Guardalavaca.
Banes. Holguín
Phone: (53 24) 3-0180

Azúcar
Bar
Hotel Sol Río de Luna y Mares.
Rafael Freyre. Holguín
Phone: (53 24) 3-0030

La Roca
Disco
Playa Guardalavaca.
Banes. Holguín
Phone: (53 24) 3-0167

Bariay
Nightclub
Hotel Sol Río de Luna y Mares.
Rafael Freyre. Holguín
Phone: (53 24) 3-0030

La Rueda
Bar
Playa Guardalavaca.
Banes. Holguín

Beach Bar
Beach bar
Hotel Playa Costa Verde.
Rafael Freyre. Holguín
Phone: (53 24) 3-0520

La Santa María
Snack bar
Hotel Atlántico-Guardalavaca.
Banes. Holguín
Phone: (53 24) 3-0180

El Capuccino
Bar
Hotel Guardalavaca.
Banes. Holguín
Phone: (53 24) 3-0218

La Tinaja
Bar
Hotel Guardalavaca.
Banes. Holguín
Phone: (53 24) 30-218

El Dorado
Lobby bar
Hotel Sol Río de Luna y Mares.
Rafael Freyre. Holguín
Phone: (53 24) 3-0030

Laguna Azul
Snack bar
Hotel Blau Costa Verde.
Rafael Freyre. Holguín
Phone: (53 24) 3-0510

El Patio
Bar
Hotel Guardalavaca.
Banes. Holguín
Phone: (53 24) 30-218

NIGHTLIFE
(HOLGUÍN)

Las Guanas
Snack bar
Playa Esmeralda.
Rafael Freyre. Holguín
Phone: (53 24) 30132

El Ranchón
Snack bar
Hotel Guardalavaca.
Banes. Holguín
Phone: (53 24) 3-0218

Lobby Bar
Lobby bar
Hotel Playa Costa Verde.
Rafael Freyre. Holguín
Phone: (53 24) 3-0520

El Saltón
Pool bar
Hotel Paradisus Río de Oro.
Rafael Freyre. Holguín
Phone: (53 24) 3-0090

Los Amigos
Bar
Playa Guardalavaca.
Banes. Holguín

El Zaguán
Bar
Hotel Guardalavaca.
Banes. Holguín
Phone: (53 24) 30-218

Oasis
Snack bar
Playa Esmeralda.
Rafael Freyre. Holguín
Phone: (53 24) 30132

Fun Pub La Conga
Disco
Hotel Paradisus Río de Oro.
Rafael Freyre. Holguín
Phone: (53 24) 30090

Palma Real
Lobby bar
Hotel Paradisus Río de Oro.
Rafael Freyre. Holguín
Phone: (53 24) 3-0090

Galileo
Snack bar
Hotel Sol Río de Luna y Mares.
Rafael Freyre. Holguín
Phone: (53 24) 3-0030

Yaguajay
Snack bar
Hotel Atlántico-Guardalavaca.
Banes. Holguín
Phone: (53 24) 3-0195

Pool Bar
Pool bar
Hotel Playa Costa Verde.
Rafael Freyre. Holguín
Phone: (53 24) 3-0520

Grill Conuco
Bar
Hotel Playa Costa Verde.
Rafael Freyre. Holguín
Phone: (53 24) 3-0520

El Tejado
Lobby bar
Hotel Guardalavaca.
Banes. Holguín
Phone: (53 24) 3-0218

Night Club Bar
Nightclub
Hotel Playa Costa Verde.
Rafael Freyre. Holguín
Phone: (53 24) 3-0520

NIGHTLIFE
(CAYO LASRGO DEL SUR)

Aqua-Bar
Bar
Villa Coral, Cayo Largo
del Sur. Isla de la Juventud
Phone: (53 45) 248-111

Medusa
Bar
Hotel Isla del Sur, Cayo Largo
del Sur. Isla de la Juventud
Phone: (53 45) 248-111

Bar de Olga
Bar
Villa Capricho, Cayo Largo
del Sur. Isla de la Juventud
Phone: (53 45) 248-111

Opalino
Bar
Hotel Barceló Cayo Largo Beach
Resort. Isla de la Juventud
Phone: (53 45) 248-080

Carey
Bar
Villa Iguana, Cayo Largo del
Sur. Isla de la Juventud
Phone: (53 45) 248-111

Opalino
Snack bar
Hotel Barceló Cayo Largo Beach
Resort. Isla de la Juventud
Phone: (53 45) 248-080

Cayo Rico
Bar
Marina Cayo Largo del Sur.
Isla de la Juventud
Phone: (53 45) 248-212

Rent a Car
Bar
Hotel Isla del Sur, Cayo Largo
del Sur. Isla de la Juventud
Phone: (53 45) 248-111

Chiringuito de Playa
Beach bar
Hotel Sol Cayo Largo.
Isla de la Juventud
Phone: (53 45) 248-260

Sirena
Bar
Marina Cayo Largo del Sur.
Isla de la Juventud
Phone: (53 45) 248-212

Daiquirí
Bar
Hotel Barceló Cayo Largo Beach
Resort. Isla de la Juventud
Phone: (53 45) 248-080

Solazul
Pool bar
Hotel Sol Cayo Largo.
Isla de la Juventud
Phone: (53 45) 248-260

El Catey
Lobby bar
Hotel Sol Pelícano.
Isla de la Juventud
Phone: (53 45) 248-333

Taberna del Pirata
Bar
Marina Cayo Largo del Sur.
Isla de la Juventud
Phone: (53 45) 248-212

El Cayito
Lobby bar
Hotel Sol Cayo Largo.
Isla de la Juventud
Phone: (53 45) 248-260

Velamar
Beach bar
Hotel Barceló Cayo Largo Beach
Resort. Isla de la Juventud
Phone: (53 45) 248-080

Karaoke Marimba
Karaoke
Hotel Sol Cayo Largo.
Isla de la Juventud
Phone: (53 45) 248-260

Zun Zun
Bar
Hotel Sol Pelícano.
Isla de la Juventud
Phone: (53 45) 248-333

Los Quelonios
Bar
Hotel Sol Pelícano.
Isla de la Juventud
Phone: (53 45) 248-333

NIGHTLIFE
(TRINIDAD)

1514
Bar
Hotel Trinidad del Mar.
Trinidad. Sancti Spiritus
Phone: (53 41) 99-6500

Lobby Bar
Bar
Hotel Costasur.
Trinidad. Sancti Spiritus
Phone: (53 41) 99-6174

Ayala
Disco
Hotel Las Cuevas.
Trinidad. Sancti Spiritus
Phone: (53 41) 99-6133

Los Cobos
Snack bar
Hotel Trinidad del Mar.
Trinidad. Sancti Spiritus
Phone: (53 41) 99-6500

Caracol
Beach bar
Hotel Costasur.
Trinidad. Sancti Spiritus
Phone: (53 41) 99-6174

Los Corsarios
Lobby bar
Hotel Ancón.
Trinidad. Sancti Spiritus
Phone: (53 41) 99-6120

Caribbean Club
Disco
Hotel Ancón.
Trinidad. Sancti Spiritus
Phone: (53 41) 99-6120

Los Galeones
Lobby bar
Hotel Trinidad del Mar.
Trinidad. Sancti Spiritus
Phone: (53 41) 99-6500

Coco Bar
Bar
Hotel Ancón.
Trinidad. Sancti Spiritus
Phone: (53 41) 99-6120

Los Galeones
Pool bar
Hotel Ancón.
Trinidad. Sancti Spiritus
Phone: (53 41) 99-6120

Costasur
Disco
Hotel Costasur.
Trinidad. Sancti Spiritus
Phone: (53 41) 99-6174

Mesón del Regidor
Bar
Calle Simón Bolívar No. 312.
Trinidad. Sancti Spiritus

El Gallo
Bar
Finca Ma´ Dolores.
Sancti Spiritus
Phone: (53 41) 99-6481

Piano Bar-Karaoke
Karaoke
Hotel Trinidad del Mar.
Trinidad. Sancti Spiritus
Phone: (53 41) 99-6500

El Potro
Bar
Finca Ma´ Dolores.
Trinidad. Sancti Spiritus
Phone: (53 41) 99-6481

Ranchón Havana Club
Bar
Hotel Ancón. Trinidad.
Phone: (53 41) 99-6120

La Manta
Bar
Hotel Costasur. Trinidad.
Phone: (53 41) 99-6174

Ranchón Playa
Beach bar
Hotel Ancón. Trinidad.
Phone: (53 41) 99-6120

Langostino
Pool bar
Hotel Costasur.
Trinidad. Sancti Spiritus
Phone: (53 41) 99-6174

Rondeño
Bar
Hotel La Ronda. Trinidad.
Phone: (53 41) 99-4011

Lina
Bar
Hotel Costasur. Trinidad.
Phone: (53 41) 99-6174

Taberna La Canchánchara
Bar
Calle Ruben Martínez Villena
esq. a Pablo Pichs. Trinidad.
Phone: (53 41) 99-4345

NIGHTLIFE
(SOROA, LAS TERRAZAS & VIÑALES)

Castillo

Bar

Villa Soroa.

Candelaria. Artemisa

Phone: (53 48) 52-3534

Salto

Bar

Villa Soroa.

Candelaria. Artemisa

Phone: (53 48) 52-3534

Centro

Bar

Villa Soroa.

Candelaria. Artemisa

Phone: (53 48) 52-3534

Snack Bar Piscina

Pool bar

Villa Soroa.

Candelaria. Artemisa

Phone: (53 48) 52-3534

Lobby Bar

Lobby bar

Villa Soroa.

Candelaria. Artemisa

Phone: (53 48) 52-3534

Amanecer del Valle

Snack bar

Hotel Los Jazmines.

Viñales. Pinar del Río

Phone: (53 48) 796205

Bar Piscina

Pool bar

Villa Aguas Claras.

Viñales. Pinar del Río

Phone: (53 48) 27-8426

Las Arcadas

Bar

Hotel Rancho San Vicente.

Viñales. Pinar del Río

Phone: (53 48) 796205

Cuevas de Viñales

Disco

Carretera a Puerto Esperanza

km. 36. Viñales. Pinar del Río

Phone: (53 48) 79-3203

Mirador

Bar

Hotel Los Jazmines.

Viñales. Pinar del Río

Phone: (53 48) 796205

Discoteca

Disco

Villa Aguas Claras.

Viñales. Pinar del Río

Phone: (53 48) 27-8426

Ranchón San Vicente

Bar

Carretera a Puerto Esperanza

km. 38. Viñales. Pinar del Río

Phone: (53 82) 79-3200

Snack Bar

Snack bar

Hotel La Ermita.

Viñales. Pinar del Río

Phone: (53 48) 796072

La Salsa

Disco

Hotel Los Jazmines.

Viñales. Pinar del Río

Phone: (53 48) 79-6205

Vista al Valle

Bar

Hotel Los Jazmines.

Viñales. Pinar del Río

Phone: (53 48) 796205

Jurásico

Bar

Villa Dos Hermanas.

Viñales. Pinar del Río

Phone: (53 48) 93223

La Terraza

Bar

Hotel La Ermita.

Viñales. Pinar del Río

Phone: (53 48) 796072

ATTRACTIONS
(VARADERO)

Amphitheater of Varadero
Theaters
Vía Blanca y carretera de
Cárdenas. Cárdenas. Matanzas

**Iglesia Presbiteriana
Reformada**
Churches-Places of Cult
Calle 34 e/ 1ra. y 2da.
Cárdenas. Matanzas

Cueva de Ambrosio
Caverns
Varadero. Cárdenas. Matanzas

Josone Park
Places of Interest
Calle 1ra. y 56. Cárdenas.
Matanzas

**Municipal Museum
of History**
Museums
Calle 57 No. 1 esq. a Playa.
Cárdenas. Matanzas
Phone: (53 45) 61-3189

**Iglesia de Nuestra
Señora de Fátima**
Churches-Places of Cult
Calle 1ra. No. 801 e/ 8 y 9.
Cárdenas. Matanzas

**Plaza América
Convention Center**
Institutions
Autopista Sur km. 11.
Cárdenas. Matanzas
Phone: (53 45) 66-7895

**Iglesia del Inmaculado
Corazón de María
(Santa Elvira)**
Churches-Places of Cult
Ave. 1ra. No. 4604 e/ 46 y 47.
Cárdenas. Matanzas

Varadero Golf Club
Places of Interest
Carretera Las Américas.
Cárdenas. Matanzas
Phone: (53 45) 66-8482

**Cueva de los Musulmanes
(The Cave of Muslims)**
Caverns
Cárdenas. Matanzas

ATTRACTIONS
(HAVANA COLONIAL)

Gun Smith's Museum
Museums
Calle Mercaderes No. 157 e/
Lamparilla y Obrapía.
La Habana Vieja. La Habana
Phone: (53 7) 861-8080

Indian Fountain
Places of Interest
Paseo del Prado y Dragones.
La Habana Vieja. La Habana

**"Santa Clara de Asis"
Convent & Church**
Places of Interest
Calle Cuba No. 602 e/ Luz y Sol.
La Habana Vieja. La Habana

Inglaterra Hotel
Monuments
Paseo del Prado e/ San Rafael y
San Miguel. La Habana Vieja.
La Habana

"Simón Bolívar" House
Museums
Calle Mercaderes No. 156 e/
Obrapía y Lamparilla.
La Habana Vieja. La Habana
Phone: (53 7) 861-3988

Instituto Cubano del Libro
Institutions
Calle O'Reilly No. 4 esq. a
Tacón. La Habana Vieja.
Phone: (53 7) 862-8091

ATTRACTIONS
(HAVANA COLONIAL)

Alameda de Paula Promenade
Places of Interest
Alameda de Paula.
La Habana Vieja. La Habana

José Martí's House
Museums
Calle Leonor Pérez (Paula)
No. 314 e/ Picota y Egido.
La Habana Vieja. La Habana
Phone: (53 7) 861-3778

Aldama Palace
Places of Interest
Calles Amistad, Reina, Aguila
y Enrique Barnet. La Habana
Vieja. La Habana

La Acacia Gallery
Art Galleries
Calle San José No. 114 e/
Industria y Consulado.
Centro Habana. La Habana
Phone: (53 7) 861-3533

Alejo Carpentier Foundation
Institutions
Calle Empedrado No. 215.
La Habana Vieja. La Habana
Phone: (53 7) 861-3667

La Casona Gallery
Art Galleries
Calle Muralla No. 107 esq. a
San Ignacio. La Habana Vieja.
Phone: (53 7) 862-2633

La Junta Locomotive
Monuments
Calle Egido, Estación Central
de Ferrocarriles de La Habana.
La Habana Vieja. La Habana

Aquarium of Old Havana
Places of Interest
Calle Teniente Rey No. 9 e/
Oficios y Mercaderes.
La Habana Vieja. La Habana
Phone: (53 7) 863-9493

La Merced Church
Churches-Places of Cult
Calle Cuba No. 806 esq. a
Merced. La Habana Vieja.
Phone: (53 7) 863-8873

Arabian House
Museums
Calle Oficios No. 16 e/ Obispo
y Obrapía. La Habana Vieja.
La Habana
Phone: (53 7) 861-5868

Lions Fountain
Places of Interest
Plaza de San Francisco de Asís.
La Habana Vieja. La Habana

Archaeological Park
Places of Interest
La Habana Vieja. La Habana

Luz y Caballero Park
Parks
La Habana Vieja. La Habana

Artistic Ceramic Museum
Museums
Calle Mercaderes No. 15 e/
Amargura y Lamparilla. La
Habana Vieja. La Habana
Phone: (53 7) 861-6130

Marquis de Arcos' House
Places of Interest
Calle Mercaderes No. 16 e/
Empedrado y O'Reilly.
La Habana Vieja. La Habana

Asian House
Museums
Calle Mercaderes No. 111 e/
Obispo y Obrapía. La Habana
Vieja. La Habana
Phone: (53 7) 863-9740

Medical Students Memorial
Monuments
Paseo del Prado y Malecón.
La Habana Vieja. La Habana

Asturian Center
Museums
Calle O'Reilly e/ Zulueta y
Monserrate. La Habana Vieja.

Monument to Santo Domingo Convent (Royal and Pontifical University of San Geronimo of Havana)
Monuments
Calle Obispo esq. a Mercaderes.
La Habana Vieja. La Habana

ATTRACTIONS
(HAVANA COLONIAL)

Bacardi Building
Places of Interest
Calle Monserrate y San Juan
de Dios. La Habana Vieja.
La Habana

Museo de las Finanzas
Museums
Calle Obispo No. 26 esq. a Cuba
La Habana Vieja. La Habana
Phone: (53 7) 862-9962

**Basilica of Saint Francis
of Assisi**
Places of Interest
Calle Oficios e/ Amargura y
Churruca. La Habana Vieja.
Phone: (53 7) 862-9683

Museo de los Orishas
Museums
Paseo del Prado No. 615 e/
Monte y Dragones.
La Habana Vieja. La Habana
Phone: (53 7) 863-5953

Car Museum
Museums
Calle Oficios No. 12 y Callejón
de Jústiz. La Habana Vieja.
Phone: (53 7) 861-5062

Museo del Naipe
Museums
Calle Muralla No. 101 esq. a
Inquisidor. La Habana Vieja.

Carlos Manuel de Céspede
Monuments
Plaza de Armas. La Habana
Vieja. La Habana

Museum of Archaeology
Museums
Calle Tacón No. 12 e/ O´Reilly y
Empedrado. La Habana Vieja.
La Habana
Phone: (53 7) 861-4469

**Castillo de los Tres Reyes
del Morro (Castle of the
Three Kings of El Morro)**
Places of Interest
Ribera este del canal de entrada
a la bahía de La Habana.
La Habana del Este. La Habana

Museum of Cigar
Museums
Calle Mercaderes No. 120 e/
Obispo y Obrapía. La Habana
Vieja. La Habana

Cathedral of Havana
Churches-Places of Cult
Calle Empedrado No. 158 e/
Mercaderes y San Ignacio.
La Habana Vieja. La Habana
Phone: (53 7) 861-7771

Museum of Colonial Art
Museums
Calle San Ignacio No. 61 e/
Empedrado y O´Reilly, Plaza
de la Catedral. La Habana Vieja.
La Habana
Phone: (53 7) 862-6440

Cathedral Square
Places of Interest
Calle Empedrado y San Ignacio.
La Habana Vieja. La Habana

**Museum of Command
Headquarters**
Museums
Fortaleza de La Cabaña.
La Habana del Este. La Habana

**Center for Contemporary
Arts "Wilfredo Lam"**
Institutions
Calle San Ignacio No. 22 esq. a
Empedrado. La Habana Vieja.
La Habana
Phone: (53 7) 861-3419

Museum of Religious Art
Museums
Calle Oficios e/ Amargura y
Churruca. La Habana Vieja.
La Habana
Phone: (53 7) 862-9683

Central Park
Parks
Paseo del Prado. La Habana
Vieja. La Habana

Museum of Rum
Museums
Calle San Pedro No. 262 e/ Sol y
Muralla. La Habana Vieja.
La Habana
Phone: (53 7) 861-8051

Central Railroad Station
Places of Interest
Calle Egido y Arsenal.
La Habana Vieja. La Habana

ATTRACTIONS
(HAVANA COLONIAL)

Museum of the City
Museums
Calle Tacón No. 1 e/ Obispo
y O'Reilly. La Habana Vieja.
Phone: (53 7) 861-2876

**Centro Cultural
Pablo de la Torriente Brau**
Institutions
Calle Muralla No. 63 e/ Oficios e
Inquisidor. La Habana Vieja.
Phone: (53 7) 66-6585

Museum of the Revolution
Museums
Calle Refugio No. 1 e/
Monserrate y Zulueta.
La Habana Vieja. La Habana
Phone: (53 7) 862-4091

**Centro Gallego-Great
Theater of Havana**
Places of Interest
Paseo del Prado e/ San Rafael
y San José. Centro Habana.
Phone: (53 7) 861-3078

National Capitol Hill
Places of Interest
Paseo del Prado e/ Dragones
y San José. La Habana Vieja.
La Habana

Church of the Holy Ghost
Churches-Places of Cult
Calle Cuba e/ Acosta y Jesús
María. La Habana Vieja.
La Habana

**National Center for
Preservation, Restoration
and Museology
CENCREM)**
Institutions
Calle Cuba No. 610 e/ Sol y Luz.
La Habana Vieja. La Habana
Phone: (53 7) 861-2877

**Convención Bautista
Cuba Occidental**
Churches-Places of Cult
Calle Zulueta No. 502 esq. a
Dragones. La Habana Vieja.

**National Museum of
Fine Arts**
Museums
Calle Trocadero e/ Zulueta y
Monserrate. La Habana Vieja.
Phone: (53 7) 862-1643

De la Real Fuerza Castle
Places of Interest
Calle O'Reilly No. 2 e/ Ave.
del Puerto y Tacón.
La Habana Vieja. La Habana
Phone: (53 7) 861-6130

**National Museum
of Music**
Museums
Calle Capdevila No. 1 e/ Aguiar
y Habana. La Habana Vieja.
Phone: (53 7) 861-9846

El Templete
Places of Interest
Calle Baratillo e/ O'Reilly y
Enna, Plaza de Armas.
La Habana Vieja. La Habana

**National Museum of
Natural History**
Museums
Calle Obispo No. 61 esq. a
Oficios. La Habana Vieja.
La Habana
Phone: (53 7) 862-0353

Fernando VII Monument
Monuments
Calle O'Reilly, Plaza de Armas.
La Habana Vieja. La Habana

Neptune Fountain
Places of Interest
Avenida del Puerto.
La Habana Vieja. La Habana

Firemen's House
Museums
Calle Mercaderes No. 162 esq. a
Lamparilla. La Habana Vieja.
La Habana

Numismatic Museum
Museums
Calle Obispo No. 310 e/ Aguiar
y Habana. La Habana Vieja.
Phone: (53 7) 861-5811

Forma Gallery
Art Galleries
Calle Obispo No. 255 e/ Cuba
y Aguiar. La Habana Vieja.
La Habana
Phone: (53 7) 862-0123

Fraternity Park
Parks
Calle Monte.
La Habana Vieja.

ATTRACTIONS
(HAVANA COLONIAL)

Old Havana and its Colonial Fortress System
World Heritage Sites
La Habana Vieja. La Habana

Francisco Albear Park
Parks
Calle Monserrate e/ Obispo
y O'Reilly. La Habana Vieja.
La Habana

Old San Francisco de Sales' School
Places of Interest
Calle Oficios No. 6 esq. a Obispo
La Habana Vieja. La Habana

Old Villa of San Cristobal of Havana
Urban Historic Centers
La Habana Vieja.

Generals of the Army Palace
Places of Interest
Calle Tacón e/ Obispo y O'Reilly
La Habana Vieja. La Habana

Plaza de Armas (Parade Ground)
Parks
Calles Tacón, Obispo, Baratillo y
O'Reilly. La Habana Vieja.
La Habana

Prado Promenade
Places of Interest
Paseo del Prado.
La Habana Vieja. La Habana

Granma Memorial
Museums
Calle Refugio No. 1 e/
Monserrate y Zulueta. La
Habana Vieja. La Habana

Plaza Vieja (Old Square)
Parks
Calles San Ignacio, Teniente Rey
Mercaderes y Muralla. La
Habana Vieja. La Habana

Guayasamin Foundation House
Art Galleries
Calle Obrapía No. 112 e/ Oficios
y Mercaderes. La Habana Vieja.
La Habana
Phone: (53 7) 861-3843

Havana Customs House
Places of Interest
Calle San Pedro. La Habana
Vieja. La Habana

Real Fábrica de Tabacos "La Corona"
Places of Interest
Calle Zulueta No. 106 e/ Refugio
y Colón. La Habana Vieja.
La Habana

Historical Museum of Sciences "Carlos J. Finlay"
Museums
Calle Cuba No. 460 e/ Amargura
y Teniente Rey.
La Habana Vieja. La Habana
Phone: (53 7) 863-4824

Remains of the Wall of Havana
Places of Interest
La Habana Vieja.
La Habana Vieja. La Habana

Historical-Military Park Morro-Cabaña
Places of Interest
Carretera de La Cabaña.
La Habana del Este. La Habana
Phone: (53 7) 862-0607

Roberto Diago Gallery
Art Galleries
Calle Muralla No. 107 esq. a San
Ignacio. La Habana Vieja.
Phone: (53 7) 862-2377

Horacio Ruíz Gallery
Art Galleries
Calle Tacón No. 4 / O'Reilly y
Empedrado. La Habana Vieja.

San Agustín Church
Churches-Places of Cult
Calle Cuba esq. a Amargura.
La Habana Vieja. La Habana

House of Africa
Museums
Calle Obrapía No. 157 e/
Mercaderes y San Ignacio.
La Habana Vieja. La Habana
Phone: (53 7) 861-5798

House of Alejandro de Humboldt
Museums
Calle Oficios No. 254 esq. a
Muralla. La Habana Vieja.

ATTRACTIONS
(HAVANA COLONIAL)

San Carlos and San Ambrosio Seminary
Places of Interest
Calle San Ignacio No. 5 e/
Empedrado y Tacón.
La Habana Vieja. La Habana

San Carlos de la Cabaña Fort
Places of Interest
Ribera este del canal de entrada
a la bahía de La Habana.
La Habana del Este. La Habana

House of Benito Juarez: Distinguished personality of Las Americas
Museums
Calle Obrapía No. 116 esq. a
Mercaderes. La Habana Vieja.
Phone: (53 7) 861-8166

San Francisco de Paula Church
Places of Interest
Calle Paula No. 9 esq. a San
Ignacio. La Habana Vieja.
La Habana

House of Carmen Montilla
Art Galleries
Calle Oficios e/ Amargura y
Teniente Rey. La Habana Vieja.
La Habana
Phone: (53 7) 33-8768

San Francisco Square
Parks
Calles Oficios, Amargura y San
Pedro. La Habana Vieja.
La Habana

House of Count Pedroso
Places of Interest
Calle San Ignacio y Empedrado.
La Habana Vieja. La Habana

San Salvador de la Punta Castle
Places of Interest
Ave. del Puerto y Paseo del
Prado. La Habana Vieja.
La Habana

House of La Obra Pía
Museums
Calle Obrapía No. 158 esq. a
Mercaderes. La Habana Vieja.
La Habana
Phone: (53 7) 861-3097

Santa Teresa de Jesus Convent & Church (Maria Auxiliadora
Churches-Places of Cult
Calle Compostela esq. a
Teniente Rey. La Habana Vieja.
La Habana
Phone: (53 7) 861-1446

House of Poetry
Institutions
Calle Muralla e/ Oficios e
Inquisidor. La Habana Vieja.
La Habana

Santo Cristo del Buen Viaje Church
Churches-Places of Cult
Calle Villegas e/ Lamparilla y
Teniente Rey. La Habana Vieja.
La Habana
Phone: (53 7) 863-1767

House of Silver Work
Museums
Calle Obispo No. 113 e/ Oficios y
Mercaderes. La Habana Vieja.
La Habana
Phone: (53 7) 863-9861

Segundo Cabo Palace
Places of Interest
Calle O'Reilly No. 4 esq. a
Tacón. La Habana Vieja.

House of the Count Casa Barreto
Places of Interest
Calle Oficios No. 362 esq. a Luz.
La Habana Vieja. La Habana

Taquechel Pharmacy Museum
Museums
Calle Obispo No. 155 e/ San
Ignacio y Mercaderes. La
Habana Vieja. La Habana

House of the Count Casa Lombillo
Places of Interest
Calle San Ignacio No. 364 e/
Teniente Rey y Muralla. La
Habana Vieja. La Habana

Terminal de Cruceros
Places of Interest
Ave. San Pedro.
La Habana Vieja. La Habana

The Christ of Havana
Places of Interest
Bahía de La Habana.
La Habana del Este. La Habana

ATTRACTIONS
(HAVANA COLONIAL)

House of the Count San Juan de Jaruco
Places of Interest
Calle Muralla esq. a San Ignacio.
La Habana Vieja. La Habana

House of the Marquis of Aguas Claras
Places of Interest
Calle San Ignacio No. 54 esq. a
Empedrado. La Habana Vieja.
La Habana

The Great Statue of the Republic
Places of Interest
Capitolio de La Habana, Paseo
del Prado y Teniente Rey.
La Habana Vieja. La Habana

Victor Manuel Gallery
Art Galleries
Calle San Ignacio No. 56, Plaza
de la Catedral. La Habana Vieja.
Phone: (53 7) 861-2955

Iglesia del Santo Angel Custodio
Churches-Places of Cult
Calle Compostela No. 2 e/
Chacón y Cuarteles. La Habana
Vieja. La Habana
Phone: (53 7) 861-0469

House of the Recio Family
Places of Interest
Calle Obispo e/ Mercaderes y
Oficios. La Habana Vieja.
La Habana

The Traditional Malecon of the City of Havana
Places of Interest
Ave. Antonio Maceo. La Habana
Vieja. La Habana

Iglesia del Sagrado Corazón de Jesús y San Ignacio de Loyola
Churches-Places of Cult
Calle Reina No. 463. Centro
Habana. La Habana

ATTRACTIONS
(HAVANA CITY)

"Amadeo Roldan" Theater & Auditorium
Theaters
Calle Calzada No. 512 esq. a D,
Vedado. Plaza de la Revolución.
Phone: (53 7) 832-1168

Iglesia de Jesús de Miramar
Churches-Places of Cult
5ta Ave. esq. a 82, Miramar.
Playa. La Habana
Phone: (53 7) 203-5301

"José Martí" Revolution Square
Places of Interest
Calle Paseo. Plaza de la
Revolución. La Habana

Iglesia de San Antonio de Padua
Churches-Places of Cult
5ta. Ave. esq. a 60, Miramar.
Playa. La Habana
Phone: (53 7) 203-5045

"Abel Santamaria's House" Museum
Museums
Calle 25 esq. a O, Vedado.
Plaza de la Revolución.
Phone: (53 7) 870-0417

Iglesia de San Juan Bosco
Churches-Places of Cult
Calle Santa Catalina No. 674 esq.
a Goss. Diez de Octubre.
La Habana
Phone: (53 7) 41-5405

ATTRACTIONS
(HAVANA CITY)

"Buendia" Theater
Theaters
Calle Loma esq. a 39, Nuevo
Vedado. Plaza de la Revolución.
La Habana
Phone: (53 7) 881-6689

Iglesia del Carmelo
Churches-Places of Cult
Calle Línea No. 1114, Vedado.
Plaza de la Revolución.
La Habana
Phone: (53 7) 833-4789

Cristobal Colon Cemetery
Monuments
Calle Zapata esq. a 12, Vedado.
Plaza de la Revolución.
La Habana

Iglesia del Corpus Christi
Churches-Places of Cult
Calle 146 No. 904 esq. a 9na.,
Reparto Cubanacán. Playa. La
Habana
Phone: (53 7) 33-7175

"El Huron Azul" Museum
Museums
Calle Paz e/ Lindero y
Constancia, Reparto Párraga.
Arroyo Naranjo. La Habana
Phone: (53 7) 57-8246

Iglesia del Nazareno
Churches-Places of Cult
Ave. 47 No. 5414. La Lisa. La
Habana
Phone: (53 7) 202-2922

"El Sotano" Theater
Theaters
Calle K e/ 25 y 27, Vedado.
Plaza de la Revolución.
Phone: (53 7) 832-0630

Iglesia del Nazareno
Churches-Places of Cult
Ave. 56 No. 5112. Marianao.
La Habana

**"Felipe Poey" Natural
History Museum**
Museums
Universidad de La Habana,
Edificio "Felipe Poey"
Plaza de la Revolución.
La Habana

**Iglesia del Sagrado
Corazón de Jesús**
Churches-Places of Cult
Calle Línea e/ C y D, Vedado.
Plaza de la Revolución.
La Habana
Phone: (53 7) 832-6807

**"Haydee Santamaria"
Gallery of Latin American
Art**
Art Galleries
Calle G e/ 3ra. y 5ta., Vedado.
Plaza de la Revolución.
Phone: (53 7) 832-4653

**Iglesia Episcopal de Cuba
(Diócesis Anglicana)**
Churches-Places of Cult
Calle 6 No. 273 e/ 11 y 13,
Plaza de la Revolución.

"Hubert de Blank" Theater
Theaters
Calle Calzada e/ A y B, Vedado.
Plaza de la Revolución.
La Habana
Phone: (53 7) 833-5962

**Iglesia Evangélica
Pentecostal (Asamblea de
Dios)**
Churches-Places of Cult
Calle Infanta esq. a Santa Marta.
Centro Habana. La Habana
Phone: (53 7) 870-0350

**"Jose Marti" Memorial
Museum**
Museums
Calle Paseo y Ave.
Independencia. Plaza de la
Revolución. La Habana
Phone: (53 7) 882-0906

Iglesia Metodista
Churches-Places of Cult
Calle 292 No. 309, Santa Fe.
Playa. La Habana

"Karl Marx" Theater
Theaters
Calle 1ra. e/ 8 y 10, Miramar.
Playa. La Habana
Phone: (53 7) 203-0801

**Iglesia Metodista Central
de La Habana**
Churches-Places of Cult
Calle Virtudes No. 152 e/ Crespo
e Industria. Centro Habana.
La Habana

ATTRACTIONS
(HAVANA CITY)

Máximo Gómez Museum
Museums
Ave. Salvador Allende, Quinta
de los Molinos. Plaza de la
Revolución. La Habana
Phone: (53 7) 879-8850

Iglesia Metodista de Cuba
Churches-Places of Cult
Calle K No. 502 esq. a 25,
Vedado. Plaza de la Revolución.
Phone: (53 7) 832-0770

"Mella" Theater
Theaters
Calle Línea No. 657 e/ A y B,
Vedado. Plaza de la Revolución.
Phone: (53 7) 833-5651

**Iglesia Presbiteriana
Reformada**
Churches-Places of Cult
Calle Reforma No. 560, Luyanó.
Diez de Octubre. La Habana
Phone: (53 7) 33-9621

**Montane Anthropological
Museum**
Museums
Universidad de La Habana,
Edificio "Felipe Poey"
Plaza de la Revolución.
Phone: (53 7) 879-3488

**Instituto Cubano de la
Música**
Institutions
Calle 15 No. 452 e/ E y F,
Vedado. Plaza de la Revolución.
Phone: (53 7) 832-3503

**"Santa Maria del Rosario"
Church**
Churches-Places of Cult
Calle 24 e/ 31 y 33, Santa María
del Rosario. Cotorro. La Habana

**Jardín Zoológico de
La Habana**
Places of Interest
Ave. 26 y Ave. del Zoológico.
Plaza de la Revolución.
La Habana
Phone: (53 7) 881-8915

Art Schools
Places of Interest
Reparto Cubanacán.
Playa. La Habana

La Fragua Martiana
Monuments
Calle Hospital No. 108 esq. a
Príncipe. Centro Habana.
La Habana

**Artistic and Literary High
School of Regla**
Monuments
Calle Máximo Gómez No. 153 e/
Ambron y La Piedra. Regla.
La Habana

Lenin Park
Places of Interest
Calle 100 y Cortina de la Presa.
Arroyo Naranjo. La Habana
Phone: (53 7) 44-3026

Calixto García Memorial
Monuments
Calle G y Malecón. Plaza de
la Revolución. La Habana

**Municipal Museum
of Guanabacoa**
Museums
Calle Martí No. 108 e/ Versalles y
San Antonio. Guanabacoa.
La Habana
Phone: (53 7) 97-9117

Callejón de Hammel
Places of Interest
Calle Plasencia e/ Concordia
y San Lázaro. Centro Habana.

**Municipal Museum
of Regla**
Museums
Calle Martí No. 158 e/ Facciolo y
La Piedra. Regla. La Habana
Phone: (53 7) 97-6989

**Catedral Episcopal de
la Santísima Trinidad**
Churches-Places of Cult
Calle 13 No. 876 esq. a 6,
Vedado. Plaza de la Revolución.

**Museo de Medicina
Tropical "Carlos J. Finlay"**
Museums
Instituto Medicina Topical
"Pedro Kouri", Autopista Novia
del Mediodia Km. 16. Playa.
La Habana
Phone: (53 7) 202-0430

ATTRACTIONS
(HAVANA CITY)

Center for Studies on Marti
Institutions
Calle Calzada No. 807 esq. a 4,
Vedado. Plaza de la Revolución.
Phone: (53 7) 55-2297

Museo Municipal de 10 de Octubre
Museums
Calle Vista Alegre esq. a San
Lázaro. Diez de Octubre.
La Habana
Phone: (53 7) 99-4761

Building of the Technical Military Institute Jose Marti
Monuments
Calle 45 y 66-A. Marianao.
La Habana

Museo Municipal de Boyeros
Museums
Calle 4 No. 40709 e/ 11 y 13,
Santiago de las Vegas.
Boyeros. La Habana

Centro de Investigación de la Cultura Cubana "Juan Marinello"
Institutions
Ave. Boyeros No. 63 e/ Bruzón y
Lugareño. Plaza de la
Revolución. La Habana
Phone: (53 7) 877-5770

Museo Municipal de Habana del Este
Museums
Calle 504 No. 5812 esq. a 5ta-C,
Guanabo. La Habana del Este.
Phone: (53 7) 96-4184

Centro Memorial "Dr. Martin Luther King, Jr."
Churches-Places of Cult
Ave. 53 No. 9609. Marianao.
La Habana

Museo Municipal de la Lisa
Museums
Calle 39 No. 208 e/ 206 y 208.
La Lisa. La Habana
Phone: (53 7) 26-06942

Chinese Cemetery
Monuments
Calle 26 e/ 31 y 33, Nuevo
Vedado. Plaza de la Revolución.

Museo Municipal de Marianao
Museums
Ave. 128-B No. 5704 esq. a 57.
Marianao. La Habana
Phone: (53 7) 26-09706

Church of Our Lady of Regla (Nuestra Señora de Regla)
Churches-Places of Cult
Calle Santuario e/ Máximo
Gómez y Litoral. Regla.
Phone: (53 7) 97-6228

Museo Municipal de San Miguel del Padrón
Museums
Calzada de Güines No. 19507 e/
Gabriel y Pepe Prieto. San
Miguel del Padrón. La Habana
Phone: (53 7) 91-0780

City Hall of Regla
Monuments
Calle Guaicanamar e/ Aranguren
y Céspedes. Regla. La Habana

Museo Municipal del Cerro
Museums
Calzada del Cerro No. 1852 esq.
a Peñón. Cerro. La Habana

Ciudades del Mundo Gallery
Art Galleries
Calle 25 esq. a L, Vedado. Plaza
de la Revolución. La Habana
Phone: (53 7) 832-3175

Museo Nacional de la Alfabetización
Museums
Calle 29-E esq. a 98.
Marianao. La Habana
Phone: (53 7) 260-8054

Cojimar Fort
Places of Interest
Malecón e/ Marcos y Victoria,
Cojímar. La Habana del Este.
La Habana

ATTRACTIONS
(HAVANA CITY)

Museo Nacional del Ministerio del Interior
Museums
Calle 14 e/ 5ta. y 3ra.,
Miramar. Playa. La Habana
Phone: (53 7) 202-1240

Cojimar Urban Site and its Natural Environment
Urban Historic Centers
Cojímar. La Habana del Este.

Museum of Sports History
Museums
Ave. Independencia esq. a
Bruzón. Plaza de la Revolución.
La Habana
Phone: (53 7) 881-4696

Conjunto Forklorico Nacional
Institutions
Calle 4 No. 103 e/ Calzada y 5ta.
Vedado. Plaza de la Revolución.
La Habana
Phone: (53 7) 833-4560

Museum of the Air Force
Museums
Ave. 212 e/ 29 y 31, La Coronela.
La Lisa. La Habana
Phone: (53 7) 271-7753

Consejo Nacional de las Artes Escénicas
Institutions
Calle 4 No. 257 e/ 11 y 13,
Vedado. Plaza de la Revolución.
La Habana
Phone: (53 7) 833-4581

Napoleon Museum
Museums
Calle San Miguel No. 1159 esq. a
Ronda. Centro Habana.
La Habana
Phone: (53 7) 879-1412

Consejo Nacional de las Artes Plásticas
Institutions
Calle 3ra. No. 1205, Miramar.
Plaza de la Revolución.
La Habana
Phone: (53 7) 203-8581

National Aquarium
Places of Interest
Calle 1ra. esq. a 60, Miramar.
Playa. La Habana
Phone: (53 7) 203-6401

Consejo Nacional del Patrimonio Cultural
Institutions
Calle 4 esq. a 13, Vedado. Plaza
de la Revolución. La Habana
Phone: (53 7) 833-4193

National Ballet of Cuba
Institutions
Calle Calzada No. 510 e/ D y E,
Vedado. Plaza de la Revolución.
La Habana
Phone: (53 7) 55-5442

Cuban Ludwig Foundation
Institutions
Calle 13 No. 509, Vedado. Plaza
de la Revolución. La Habana
Phone: (53 7) 832-4270

National Botanic Garden
Places of Interest
Carretera del Rocío km. 3,
Calabazar. Arroyo Naranjo.
La Habana
Phone: (53 7) 54-4108

Cuban Postal Museum
Museums
Ave. Rancho Boyeros, Ministerio
de Comunicaciones. Plaza de
la Revolución. La Habana
Phone: (53 7) 57-4150

National Museum of Decorative Arts
Museums
Calle 17 No. 502 e/ D y E,
Vedado. Plaza de la Revolución.
Phone: (53 7) 830-9848

Cultural House of Plaza Municipality
Institutions
Calle Calzada esq. a 8, Vedado.
Plaza de la Revolución.
Phone: (53 7) 831-2023

National Puppet Theater
Theaters
Calle M e/ 19 y 21, Vedado.
Plaza de la Revolución.
Phone: (53 7) 832-6262

Dance Museum
Museums
Calle Línea No. 365 esq. a G,
Vedado. Plaza de la Revolución.
La Habana
Phone: (53 7) 831-2198

ATTRACTIONS
(HAVANA CITY)

National Theater of Cuba
Theaters
Calle Paseo y 39. Plaza de la
Revolución. La Habana
Phone: (53 7) 879-6011

Ecological Reserve La Coca
Places of Interest
Campo Florida.
La Habana del Este. La Habana

National Zoo
Places of Interest
Carretera de Varona km. 2 ½,
Capdevila. Boyeros. La Habana
Phone: (53 7) 44-7613

Ermita del Potosi
Churches-Places of Cult
Calzada de Guanabacoa y
Potosí. Guanabacoa. La Habana

**Neighborhood No. 1
Camilo Cienfuegos City**
Places of Interest
Reparto Camilo Cienfuegos.
La Habana del Este. La Habana

**Ernest Hemingway
Museum**
Museums
Finca La Vigía, San Francisco de
Paula. San Miguel del Padrón.
La Habana
Phone: (53 7) 91-0809

**Farm House of the Rosell
Family**
Monuments
Calle Martí No. 308.
La Habana del Este. La Habana

**Nuestra Señora de la
Asuncion Church**
Churches-Places of Cult
Calle Pepe Antonio e/ Martí y
Cadenas. Guanabacoa.
La Habana

Expocuba
Places of Interest
Carretera del Rocío km. 3,
Calabazar. Arroyo Naranjo.
La Habana
Phone: (53 7) 44-6251

**Old Villa of Asunncion
de Guanabacoa**
Urban Historic Centers
Villa de Guanabacoa.
Guanabacoa. La Habana

Parque Almendares
Places of Interest
Calle 49-B y 47. Plaza de la
Revolución. La Habana

**Fondo Cubano de Bienes
Culturales**
Institutions
Ave. 47 No. 4702 esq. a 36,
Reparto Kohly. Playa.
La Habana
Phone: (53 7) 204-8005

**Parroquia de Nuestra
Señora del Carmen**
Churches-Places of Cult
Calle Infanta esq. a Neptuno.
Centro Habana. La Habana
Phone: (53 7) 878-5168

Fundación "Fernando Ortiz"
Institutions
Calle L No. 160 esq. a 27,
Vedado. Plaza de la Revolución.
Phone: (53 7) 832-4334

**Parroquia de San Juan
de Letrán**
Churches-Places of Cult
Calle 19 No. 258 e/ J e I, Vedado.
Plaza de la Revolución.
Phone: (53 7) 832-7329

**Fundación de la Naturaleza
y el Hombre "Antonio
Nuñez Jiménez"**
Institutions
Calle 5ta.B No. 661 e/ 66 y 70,
Miramar. Playa. La Habana
Phone: (53 7) 209-2885

**Primera Iglesia
Presbiteriana de La Habana**
Churches-Places of Cult
Calle Salud No. 222. Centro
Habana. La Habana
Phone: (53 7) 33-8410

**Fundación del Nuevo Cine
Latinoamericano**
Institutions
Calle 212 No. 21254 esq. a 31.
La Lisa. La Habana
Phone: (53 7) 271-8311

**Quinta de los Molinos
y su delimitación**
Museums
Ave. Salvador Allende. Plaza de
la Revolución. La Habana

ATTRACTIONS
(HAVANA CITY)

Gallery 23 and 12
Art Galleries
Calle 12 esq. a 23, Vedado. Plaza
de la Revolución. La Habana
Phone: (53 7) 831-3339

**Real Fábrica de Tabacos
"Partagás"**
Places of Interest
Calle Industria No. 520 e/
Dragones y Barcelona. Centro
Habana. La Habana

**Havana Convention
Center**
Institutions
Ave. 146 e/ 11 y 13, Reparto
Cubanacán. Playa. La Habana
Phone: (53 7) 203-6011

**Registro Nacional de
Bienes Culturales**
Institutions
Calle 17 No. 1009 e/ 10 y 12,
Vedado. Plaza de la Revolución.
La Habana
Phone: (53 7) 833-9658

Havana Gallery
Art Galleries
Calle Línea No. 460 e/ E y F,
Vedado. Plaza de la Revolución.
Phone: (53 7) 832-7101

**Salones de Convenciones
Hotel Nacional de Cuba**
Institutions
Calle O esq. a 21, Vedado. Plaza
de la Revolución. La Habana
Phone: (53 7) 873-3564

Havana Model
Places of Interest
Calle 28 e/ 1ra. y 3ra., Miramar.
Playa. La Habana

**San Francisco Convent
& Church**
Churches-Places of Cult
Calle San Francisco e/ Máximo
Gómez y Corral Falso.
Guanabacoa. La Habana

House for las Américas
Institutions
Calle 3ra. esq. a G, Vedado.
Plaza de la Revolución.
La Habana
Phone: (53 7) 55-2705

**San Francisco Javier de los
Quemados Church**
Churches-Places of Cult
Calle 51 No. 10620 esq. a 108-A.
Marianao. La Habana

House of Amelia Pelaez
Monuments
Calle Estrada Palma No. 261 e/
Juan Bruno Zayas y Consejal
Veiga. Diez de Octubre.
La Habana

San Lazaro Tower
Places of Interest
Malecón y Marina. Centro
Habana. La Habana

Urban area of Regla
Urban Historic Centers
Regla. La Habana

House of Antonio Castells
Monuments
Calle Flores No. 468 e/ Santa
Emilia y Zapote. Diez de
Octubre. La Habana

**Santa Dorotea de Luna
de La Chorrera Fort**
Places of Interest
Malecón e/ 18 y 29, Vedado.
Plaza de la Revolución.

**House of Dulce Maria
Loynaz**
Museums
Calle 19 No. 502 e/ E y D,
Vedado. Plaza de la Revolución.
La Habana

**Santiago de las Vegas
Parish Church**
Churches-Places of Cult
Calle 190 e/ 409 y 411, Santiago
de las Vegas. Boyeros.
La Habana

**Santuario Nacional San
Lázaro (El Rincón)**
Churches-Places of Cult
Calzada de San Antonio km. 23
½, Santiago de Las Vegas.
Boyeros. La Habana

**Santo Domingo Convent
& Church**
Churches-Places of Cult
Calle Santo Domingo e/ Roloff y
Lebredo. Guanabacoa.
La Habana

ATTRACTIONS
(SANTIAGO DE CUBA)

"Emilio Bacardi Moreau" Provincial Museum
Museums
Calle Pío Rosado 552 e/ Aguilera y Heredia. Santiago de Cuba
Phone: (53 226) 62-8402

Metropolitan Cathedral
Churches-Places of Cult
Calles Heredia, Félix Pena, Bartolomé Masó y General Lacret. Santiago de Cuba

"La Isabelica" Museum
Museums
Carretera de la Gran Piedra km. 14. Santiago de Cuba

Moncada Barracks
Places of Interest
Calles General Portuondo, Ave. de los Libertadores y Carlos Aponte. Santiago de Cuba

2da Iglesia Bautista de Cuba Oriental
Churches-Places of Cult
Calle 3ra. No. 455, Reparto Sueño. Santiago de Cuba

Municipal Historical of Santiago de Cuba
Monuments
Calle Aguilera esq. a Padre Pico.

Municipal Museum of the 3rd Front "Mario Muñoz Monroy"
Museums
III Frente. Tercer Frente. Santiago de Cuba

Abel Santamaría Park
Museums
Calles General Portuondo, Ave. de los Libertadores, Callejón América y Saturnino Lora. Santiago de Cuba
Phone: (53 226) 62-4119

Acuario Baconao
Places of Interest
Carretera Baconao km 27 1/2. Santiago de Cuba

Municipal Museum of the Contramaestre "Jesús Rabi"
Museums
Ave. 4 No. 512 e/ 5 y 7, Baire. Contramaestre. Santiago de Cuba
Phone: (53 226) 69-9339

Aguilera Park-Dolores Square
Parks
Calles Aguilera, Mayía Rodríguez y Porfirio Valiente. Santiago de Cuba

Museum of the Guamá "Combate de La Plata"
Museums
Poblado de La Plata. Guamá. Santiago de Cuba

Alameda Clock-Tower
Places of Interest
Ave. Jesús Menéndez y Aguilera. Santiago de Cuba

Municipal Museum of the Palma Soriano
Museums
Calle Martí s/n e/ Villuendas y Lora. Palma Soriano. Santiago de Cuba
Phone: (53 226) 63802

Arte Universal Gallery
Art Galleries
Calle C e/ M y Terrazas, Reparto Vista Alegre. Santiago de Cuba

Municipal Museum of the San Luis "29 de abril"
Museums
Calle Máximo Gómez No. 302 e/ Moncada y Céspedes. San Luis. Santiago de Cuba
Phone: (53 226) 62632

Arts and Crafts School Major General Antonio Maceo Grajales
Historic Sites
Santiago de Cuba

Museum of the Songo La Maya "José Maceo"
Museums
Calle Luis Bonne No. 99. Songo-La Maya. Santiago de Cuba

Bacardí Rum Company
Places of Interest
Calle Peralejo No. 3 e/ Gonzalo Quesada y Narciso López. Santiago de Cuba

ATTRACTIONS
(SANTIAGO DE CUBA)

Museo Arquidiocesano
Museums
Calle Heredia esq. a Santo
Tomás, Catedral Metropolitana
de Santiago de Cuba.
Santiago de Cuba

Baconao Park
Places of Interest
Carretera de Baconao.
Santiago de Cuba

**Museo de Ciencias
Naturales "Tomás Romay"**
Museums
Calle Enramadas s/n e/ Barnada
y Parais. Santiago de Cuba
Phone: (53 226) 62-3277

**Baconao Reserve of the
Biosphere**
Areas of Natural Interest
Baconao. Santiago de Cuba

**Museo de Historia Natural
"Valle de la Prehistoria"**
Museums
Carretera Baconao km. 6 ½.
Santiago de Cuba
Phone: (53 226) 63-9239

**Birthplace of Antonio
Maceo**
Museums
Calle Los Maceo No. 207 e/
Corona y Morúa Delgado.
Santiago de Cuba
Phone: (53 226) 62-3750

**Museo de la Guerra
Hispano-Cubano-
Norteamericana**
Museums
Carretera de Siboney km. 13 ½.
Santiago de Cuba
Phone: (53 226) 63-9119

Birthplace of Frank Pais
Museums
Calle General Banderas No. 226
e/ Habana y Maceo.
Santiago de Cuba
Phone: (53 226) 65-2710

Museo de La Imagen
Museums
Calle 8 No. 106 e/ 3 y 5, Reparto
Vista Alegre. Santiago de Cuba
Phone: (53 226) 64-2234

**Birthplace of Jose Maria
Heredia**
Museums
Calle Heredia No. 260 e/ Pío
Rosado y Hartman.
Santiago de Cuba

**Museo del Transporte
Terrestre**
Museums
Carretera Baconao km. 8 ½,
Daiquirí. Santiago de Cuba
Phone: (53 226) 63-9197

Bofill Gallery
Art Galleries
Calle Heredia e/ Pío Rosado y
Hartmann. Santiago de Cuba

**Museum Dedicated to the
Clandestine Struggle**
Museums
Calle General Rabí No. 1.
Santiago de Cuba
Phone: (53 226) 62-4689

Calle 24 de Febrero
Monuments
Calle 24 de Febrero s/n (Trocha).
Santiago de Cuba

**Museum of Cuban
Historical Background**
Museums
Calle Félix Pena No. 612 e/
Aguilera y Heredia.
Santiago de Cuba
Phone: (53 226) 65-2652

**Carlos Manuel de
Céspedes Park**
Parks
Calles Aguilera, General Lacret,
Heredia y Felix Pena.
Santiago de Cuba

Museum of Piracy
Museums
Castillo San Pedro de la Roca del
Morro. Santiago de Cuba
Phone: (53 226) 69-1569

Carnival Museum
Museums
Calle Heredia No. 303 e/ Porfirio
Valiente y Pío Rosado.
Santiago de Cuba
Phone: (53 226) 62-6955

ATTRACTIONS
(SANTIAGO DE CUBA)

Museum-Mausoleum Second Forefront (Segundo Frente)
Museums
Ave. de los Mártires s/n, Mayarí Arriba. Santiago de Cuba
Phone: (53 226) 62-5319

Casa del Caribe
Institutions
Calle 13 No. 154 esq. a 8, Reparto Vista Alegre. Santiago de Cuba
Phone: (53 226) 64-2285

Old Villa of Santiago de Cuba
Urban Historic Centers
Ciudad de Santiago de Cuba. Santiago de Cuba

Castle of San Pedro de la Roca
World Heritage Sites
Carretera de El Morro km. 8. Santiago de Cuba
Phone: (53 226) 69-1569

Oriente Gallery
Art Galleries
Calle Lacret No. 653 e/ Heredia y Aguilera. Santiago de Cuba

Centro de Estudios "Antonio Maceo"
Institutions
Calle Los Maceo No. 305 e/ San Fermín y Santo Tomás. Santiago de Cuba
Phone: (53 226) 65-2550

Our Lady of the Caridad Church (Iglesia de Nuestra Señora de la Caridad) (Natural Sanctuary of the Caridad del Cobre)
Places of Interest
Carretera al Cobre. Santiago de Cuba

Church and Monastery of St. Francis
Churches-Places of Cult
Calle Juan Bautista Sagarra No. 121 e/ Mariano Corona y Callejón del Muro. Santiago de Cuba

Palace of the Municipal Government
Places of Interest
Calle Aguilera No. 251 e/ General Lacret y Felix Pena.

Church of the Holy Family
Churches-Places of Cult
Calle 11 No. 53 e/ 6ta. y 4ta., Reparto Vista Alegre. Santiago de Cuba

Palacio de Gobierno Provincial
Places of Interest
Calle Aguilera No. 355 e/ Pío Rosado y Hartman. Santiago de Cuba

Church of the Holy Trinity
Churches-Places of Cult
Calle General Moncada No. 259 e/ José M. Gómez y General Portuondo. Santiago de Cuba

Park of Liberty-Mars Square
Parks
Calles Victoriano Garzón, Pérez Carbó, Aguilera y Plácido. Santiago de Cuba

College of St. Basil the Great
Places of Interest
Calle Bartolomé Masó No. 203 e/ Félix Pena y Mariano Corona. Santiago de Cuba

Pico Real del Turquino
Places of Interest
Sierra Maestra. Guamá.

Command Headquarters of the Second Eastern Front "Frank Pais"
Museums
Ave. Los Mártires s/n. Segundo Frente. Santiago de Cuba

Promenade of the Alameda Michaelsen
Places of Interest
Ave. Jesús Menéndez e/ Aguilera y Aduana. Santiago de Cuba

Conjunto de Ruinas de Cafetales Franceses
World Heritage Sites
Sierra Maestra. Santiago de Cuba

Residence of Adela Babun Selma
Places of Interest
Ave. Pujols No. 108 e/ Aguilera y Taíno. Santiago de Cuba

ATTRACTIONS
(SANTIAGO DE CUBA)

Convención Bautista de Cuba Oriental
Churches-Places of Cult
Calle Carnicería No. 503.
Santiago de Cuba

Residence of Alomá Family
Places of Interest
Calle Félix Pena No. 352 e/
General Portuondo y Máximo
Gómez. Santiago de Cuba

Customs Building
Places of Interest
Ave. Jesús Menéndez No. 702.
Santiago de Cuba

Residence of Carmen Brauet de Rosell
Places of Interest
Ave. Manduley No. 104 e/ 3ra. y
5ta. Santiago de Cuba

Dolores Church
Places of Interest
Calle Mayía Rodríguez No. 453
e/ Aguilera y Heredia.
Santiago de Cuba

Residence of Guillermo Castellvi
Places of Interest
Ave. Manduley No. 52 e/ 1ra. y
3ra. Santiago de Cuba

Dolores School
Places of Interest
Calle Mayía Rodríguez No. 451
e/ Aguilera y Heredia.
Santiago de Cuba

Residence of Rafael Salcedo de las Cuevas
Places of Interest
Calle Heredia No. 206-210 e/
Hartman y General Lacret.
Santiago de Cuba

El Cañón Museum
Museums
Finca San Isidro km 7, carretera
de Puerto Boniato a San Luis.
San Luis. Santiago de Cuba

Residence of the De la Torre Family
Places of Interest
Calle Heredia No. 303 e/
Porfirio Valiente y Pío Rosado.

El Uvero
Historic Sites
Carretera Granma s/n e/ Escuela
Simbólica y Campo Deportivo.
Guamá. Santiago de Cuba

Residence of the Gómez Villasana Family
Places of Interest
Calle Bartolomé Masó No. 358
e/ Pío Rosado y Hartman.
Santiago de Cuba

El Viso Fort
Parks
Carretera del Escandel.
Santiago de Cuba

Furnia del Pipe
Caverns
Baire. Contramaestre.
Santiago de Cuba

Residence of the Kindelán Family
Places of Interest
Calle Aguilera No. 468 e/ Mayía
Rodríguez y Porfirio Valiente.
Santiago de Cuba

Residence of the Learned Antonio Bravo Correoso
Places of Interest
Calle Félix Pena e/ Castillo
Duany y Santa Rita.
Santiago de Cuba

Heredia Theater
Theaters
Ave. de Las Américas e/ Ave. de
los Desfiles y Prolongación de
Angel Salazar. Santiago de Cuba

Residence of the Notó Family
Places of Interest
Calle Pío Rosado No. 358 e/
Máximo Gómez y Juan Bautista
Sagarra. Santiago de Cuba

Hermanos La Salle School
Places of Interest
Calle Heredia No. 102 e/ Félix
Pena y Corona.
Santiago de Cuba

Residence of the Schueg Family
Places of Interest
Calle Bartolomé Masó No. 354 e/
Pío Rosado y Hartman.
Santiago de Cuba

ATTRACTIONS
(SANTIAGO DE CUBA)

Historical Museum "July 26"
Museums
Calle Trinidad e/ Ave. Moncada y Carretera Central. Santiago.
Phone: (53 226) 62-0157

Residence of the Tejada Brothers
Places of Interest
Calle Heredia No. 304 e/ Porfirio Valiente y Pío Rosado. Santiago de Cuba

Historical Museum of Palma Soriano
Museums
Calle Aguilera No. 201 e/ 1ro de Mayo y Quintín Banderas. Palma Soriano.
Phone: (53 226) 63983

Residence of the Zayas Family
Places of Interest
Calle Heredia No. 266 e/ Pío Rosado y Hartman. Santiago de Cuba

House of Diego Velázquez
Places of Interest
Calle Félix Pena No. 612 e/ Aguilera y Heredia. Santiago de Cuba

Revolution Square "Major Antonio Maceo"
Monuments
Calles A, Ave. de las Américas, 9 y Carretera Central. Santiago.
Phone: (53 226) 64-3053

House of the Norma Family
Places of Interest
Calle Joaquín Castillo Duany No. 437 e/ Hartman y General Lacret. Santiago de Cuba

Royal Bivouac Prison
Places of Interest
Calle Aguilera No. 131 e/ Padre Pico y 10 de Octubre. Santiago de Cuba

Iglesia Adventista del 7mo Día en Cuba
Churches-Places of Cult
Calle K esq. a Céspedes. Santiago de Cuba

Rum Museum
Museums
Calle Bartolomé Masó No. 358 e, Pío Rosado y Hartman. Santiago de Cuba
Phone: (53 226) 62-3737

Iglesia de María Auxiliadora (Don Bosco)
Churches-Places of Cult
Calle Lorraine No. 1021.

San Lorenzo
Historic Sites
Terraplén "Los Lajeales", despulpadora "San Lorenzo". Tercer Frente. Santiago de Cuba

Iglesia Metodista
Churches-Places of Cult
Calle Lacret esq. a San Basilio. Santiago de Cuba

Iglesia de Nuestra Señora del Carmen
Churches-Places of Cult
Calle Félix Pena No. 507 e/ Tamayo Fleites y José A. Saco. Santiago de Cuba

Santa Ifigenia Cemetery
Places of Interest
Ave. Raúl Perozo s/n, Reparto Agüero. Santiago de Cuba

Iglesia del Cristo de la Salud
Churches-Places of Cult
Calle 10 de Octubre esq. a San Antonio. Santiago de Cuba

Santa Lucía Church
Churches-Places of Cult
Calle Pío Rosado No. 703 e/ J. Castillo Duany y Eduardo Yero. Santiago de Cuba

Iglesia del Cristo Rey
Churches-Places of Cult
Calle Raúl Perozo No. 130, Reparto Marimón. Santiago de Cuba

Santo Tomás Church
Churches-Places of Cult
Calle Félix Pena No. 314 e/ José Mariano Gómez y General Portuondo. Santiago de Cuba

Jíbara Cave
Caverns
Baire. Contramaestre. Santiago de Cuba

ATTRACTIONS
(SANTIAGO DE CUBA)

Iglesia Evangélica Pentecostal
Churches-Places of Cult
Paseo Martí esq. a Rizal.
Santiago de Cuba

Serrano Building
Places of Interest
Calle José A. Saco No. 208-212
e/ Félix Pena y M. Corona.
Santiago de Cuba

Social Centre of the Spanish Community
Places of Interest
Calle Heredia No. 259 e/ Pío
Rosado y Hartman.
Santiago de Cuba

Imperial Hotel
Historic Sites
Calle José A. Saco No. 251 e/
General Lacret y Félix Pena.
Santiago de Cuba

Sociedad Tumba Francesa La Caridad de Oriente
Institutions
Calle Los Maceos No. 501 esq. a
San Bartolomé, Los Hoyos.
Santiago de Cuba

St. Jerome Housing Complex
Places of Interest
Calle Sánchez Hechavarría No.
469-471-473-477 e/ Porfirio
Valiente y Pío Rosado.
Santiago de Cuba

La Estrella Fortress
Places of Interest
Carretera de Ciudamar km. 8.
Santiago de Cuba

Teacher-Training School of Oriente (Eastern part of Cuba)
Monuments
Santiago de Cuba

La Gran Piedra Natural Park
Areas of Natural Interest
La Gran Piedra.
Santiago de Cuba

The Granjita Siboney (Siboney Farm)
Museums
Carretera de Siboney km. 13 ½.
Santiago de Cuba
Phone: (53 226) 63-9168

La Milagrosa Church
Churches-Places of Cult
Calle 2da., Reparto Vista
Hermosa. Santiago de Cuba

The Great Rock
Monuments
Carretera de la Gran Piedra km.
14. Santiago de Cuba

Turquino National Park
Areas of Natural Interest
Sierra Maestra. Guamá.
Santiago de Cuba

Law Courts
Monuments
Ave. de Los Libertadores s/n e/
A y Victoriano Garzón.

Mangos de Baragua
Historic Sites
Carretera Mangos de Baraguá-
Regina. Mella. Santiago de Cuba

Velázquez´s Balcony
Places of Interest
Calle Corona No. 660 e/ Heredia
y Bartolomé Masó. Santiago

Mansion of the Bosch Family
Places of Interest
Ave. Manduley No. 254 e/ 9 y 11.
Santiago de Cuba

Wooden Architecture in Key Granma (Smith) and the vicinity
Places of Interest
Cayo Granma, bahía de Santiago
de Cuba. Santiago de Cuba

Mausoleum of José Martí
Monuments
Cementerio de Santa Ifigenia.
Santiago de Cuba

Yarayó Fort
Monuments
Ave. Crombet esq. a Juan
Gualberto Gómez.
Santiago de Cuba

ATTRACTIONS
(HOLGUÍN)

"Chorro de Maita"
Museums
Cerro de Yaguajay.
Banes. Holguín

Museo Municipal de Gibara
Museums
Calle Independencia No. 19, bajos, e/ Céspedes y J. Peralta.
Gibara. Holguín
Phone: (53 24) 4407

Bahía de Naranjo Natural Park
Areas of Natural Interest
Bahía de Naranjo. Rafael Freyre.
Holguín

Museo Municipal de Historia
Museums
Calle Thelmo Esperance No. 515
Banes. Holguín
Phone: (53 24) 3555

Bariay Bay and its natural environment
Historic Sites
Bahía de Baray.
Rafael Freyre. Holguín

Museo Municipal de Moa
Museums
Calle Mario Muñoz No. 28,
Reparto Aserrio. Moa. Holguín
Phone: (53 24) 6-4189

Portales
Caverns
Rafael Freyre. Holguín

Battery of Ferdinand VII
Historic Sites
Plaza de la Fortaleza.
Gibara. Holguín

Museo Municipal de Rafael Freyre
Museums
Calle 10 No. 39 esq. a a 9. Rafael
Freyre. Holguín
Phone: (53 24) 0336

Church of Jesus of the Mountain
Churches-Places of Cult
Carretera Holguín-Gibara km.
17, Poblado Floro Pérez. Gibara.

Museum of Decorative Arts
Museums
Calle Independencia No. 19,
altos, e/ Luz Caballero y J.
Peralta. Gibara. Holguín

Church of Our Lady of Charity
Churches-Places of Cult
Calle Martí No. 11. Banes.
Holguín

Church of St. Lucy
Churches-Places of Cult
Calle B y 3, Santa Lucía. Rafael
Freyre. Holguín

Gran Caverna de Moa
Caverns
Macizo montañoso de Moa.
Moa. Holguín

San Fulgencio de Gibara Parish Church
Churches-Places of Cult
Calles Independencia, Martí,
Sartorio y Luz Caballero.
Gibara. Holguín

Gibara "Unión Club" Colonial Theatre
Places of Interest
Calle Sartorio No. 5 e/ Peralta y
Luz Caballero. Gibara. Holguín

Sierra de los Farallones de Gran Tierra de Moa
Places of Interest
Moa. Holguín

Spanish Casino
Places of Interest
Calle Luz Caballero No. 22 e/
General Soriano e
Independencia. Gibara. Holguín

Indo-Cuban Bani Museum
Museums
Calle General Marrero No. 305 e/
Ave. José Martí y Carlos M. de
Céspedes. Banes. Holguín
Phone: (53 24) 48-2487

Tanques Azules
Caverns
Caletones. Gibara. Holguín

The Hierro Hill
Monuments
Carretera Holguín-Gibara km.
17. Gibara. Holguín

ATTRACTIONS
(TRINIDAD)

"Guamuhaya" Archeological Museum
Museums
Calle Simón Bolívar No. 457,
Plaza Mayor. Trinidad.
Phone: (53 41) 9- 3420

Iglesia y Convento de San Francisco de Paula
Places of Interest
Calle Fernando Hernández esq.
Piro Guinart. Trinidad.

Architectural Museum of Trinidad
Museums
Calle Ripalda No. 83 e/
Fernando Hernández y Ruben
Martínez Villena. Trinidad.
Phone: (53 41) 9- 3208

Municipal Museum of Trinidad (Cantero Palace)
Museums
Calle Simón Bolívar No. 423.
Trinidad. Sancti Spiritus
Phone: (53 41) 9-4460

Cabildo de los Congos Reales o de San Antonio
Places of Interest
Calle Isidro Armenteros No. 168
Trinidad. Sancti Spiritus

National Museum of the Struggle against Bandits
Museums
Calle Fernando Hernández esq.
Piro Guinart. Trinidad.
Phone: (53 419) 4121

Casa de la Cultura Trinitaria
Places of Interest
Calle Francisco J. Zerquera No.
406. Trinidad. Sancti Spiritus

Old Villa of the Holy Trinidad
Urban Historic Centers
Trinidad. Sancti Spiritus

Galería Amelia Peláez
Art Galleries
Calle Simón Bolívar No. 418.
Trinidad. Sancti Spiritus

Parish Church of Holy Trinity
Churches-Places of Cult
Calle Francisco J. Zerquera No.
456. Trinidad. Sancti Spiritus
Phone: (53 41) 9-4308

Historical Center of Trinidad and the Valley of Sugar Cane Mills
World Heritage Sites
Trinidad. Sancti Spiritus

Romantic Museum (Brunet Palace)
Museums
Calle Fernando Hernández
Echemendía No. 52, Plaza
Mayor. Trinidad. Sancti Spiritus
Phone: (53 41) 9-4363

House of Aldemán Ortiz (Art Gallery)
Art Galleries
Calle Rubén Martínez Villena
No. 43. Trinidad. Sancti Spiritus
Phone: (53 41) 9-4432

Santa Ana Church and Square
Places of Interest
Trinidad. Sancti Spiritus

Iglesia Bautista de Cuba Occidental
Churches-Places of Cult
Calle Antonio Maceo No. 4325.
Trinidad. Sancti Spiritus

Tower of the Old Sugar Cane Mill Manacas-Iznaga
Monuments
Carretera de Trinidad a Sancti
Spiritus. Trinidad. Sancti Spiritus

Iglesia de Nuestra Señora de la Candelaria (Ermita de la Popa)
Places of Interest
Trinidad. Sancti Spiritus

Valle de los Ingenios
Monuments
Trinidad. Sancti Spiritus

ATTRACTIONS
(VIÑALES)

Museo Comunidad Las Terrazas
Museums
Comunidad Las Terrazas.
Candelaria. Artemisa

Sierra del Rosario Reserve of the Biosphere
Areas of Natural Interest
Sierra del Rosario.
Candelaria. Artemisa

Orquideario de Soroa
Places of Interest
Carretera de Soroa km. 8.
Candelaria. Artemisa

Museo Municipal de Viñales "Adela Azcuy Labrador"
Museums
Calle Salvador Cisneros No. 115
e/ Adela Azcuy y Celso
Maragoto. Viñales. Pinar del Ríc
Phone: (53 82) 79-3395

Gran Caverna de Santo Tomás
Caverns
Valle de Santo Tomás. Viñales.
Pinar del Río

Cueva del Cura
Caverns
Viñales. Pinar del Río

Palmerito
Caverns
Valle de las Dos Hermanas.
Viñales. Pinar del Río

Cueva del Garrafón
Caverns
Viñales. Pinar del Río

Prehistoric Mural
Places of Interest
Valle de Viñales. Viñales.
Pinar del Río

Cueva del Indio
Caverns
Valle de Viñales. Viñales.
Pinar del Río

Viñales National Park
Areas of Natural Interest
Viñales. Pinar del Río

Viñales Town
Urban Historic Centers
Viñales. Viñales. Pinar del Río

Memorial a Los Malagones
Museums
Comunidad Moncada. Viñales.
Pinar del Río

Viñales Valley
World Heritage Sites
Sierra de los Organos. Viñales.
Pinar del Río

Museo Paleontológico
Museums
Base de campismo "Dos
Hermanas", Carretera del
Moncada al lado del Mural de
la Prehistoria. Viñales.

Cueva de los Portales
Caverns
Valle de Viñales. Los Palacios.
Pinar del Río

Caverna del Arroyo
Caverns
Viñales. Pinar del Río

PRIVATE RESTAURANTS
(HAVANA CITY)

Paladar la Fontana
Grill
Avenida 3A No 305, Playa
Phone: (537) 202-8337

Paladar Calle 10
Caribbean
Calle 10 No 314 Entre Ave 3 & 5,
Playa
Phone: (537) 205-3970

Castas y Tal
Caribbean
Calle E 158B Entre 9 & Calzada,
Vedado
Phone: (537) 833-1425

Paladar los Cactus de 33
Caribbean
Av 33 No 3405 Entre Calles 34 &
36, Playa
Phone: (537) 203-5139

Paladar Vista Mar
Seafood
Av 1 Entre Calles 22 & 24, Playa
Phone: (537) 203-8328

Paladar Torressón
Caribbean
Malecón Entre Capdevila &
Genios
Phone: (537) 861-7476

El Hurón Azul
Caribbean
Humboldt # 153, esq. P, Vedado
Phone: (537) 879-1691

Doña Juana
Caribbean
Calle 19 #909 (altos), % 6 y 8,
Vedado
Phone: (537) 832-2699

La Palma
Caribbean
Jovellar #305 % M y N, Vedado
Phone: (537) 878-3488

El Recanto
Calle 17 #957 Apt 8 % 8 y 10,
Vedado
Phone: (537) 830-4396

El Helecho
Caribbean
Calle 6 #203 % 11 y Linea,
Vedado
Phone: (537) 831-3552

Amor
Caribbean
Calle 23 #759, 3rd floor, % B y C,
Vedado
Phone: (537) 833-8150

Casa Sarasua
Caribbean
Calle 25 #510, Apt. 1, % H y I,
Vedado
Phone: (537) 832-2114

El Jinete
Caribbean
Infanta #102 esq, 25, Vedado
Phone: (537) 878-2290

Marpoly
Caribbean
Calle K #154 % 13 y 11, Vedado
Phone: (537) 832-2471

El Capitolio
Caribbean
Calle 13 #1159 % 16 y 18, Vedado
Phone: (537) 831-9251

Las 3B
Caribbean
Calle 21 % L y K, Vedado
Phone: (537) 832-9276

Balcón del Eden
Caribbean
Ave K % 19 y 21, Vedado
Phone: (537) 832-9113

Divino
International
Calle Raquel e/ Esperanza y
Lindero. Arroyo Naranjo
Phone: (537) 643-7734

Los Cascabeles
Italian
San Juan No. 2541 e/ Calzada de
Bejucal y Matanzas. Arroyo
Naranjo
Phone: (537) 643-7191

El Gallo de Oro
International
Callejón de Lucero No. 7 e/
Calzada de Managua y Santa
Hortencia. Arroyo
Naranjo
Phone: (537) 644-4382

PRIVATE RESTAURANTS
(HAVANA CITY)

Rancho Manso
International
Calzada de Managua #163 e/ 1ra
y Miguel Viondi. Arroyo
Naranjo
Phone: (535) 232-9762

Doña Teresa
International
Avenida 229 No.21011 e/ 210 y
216. Fontanar. Boyeros
Phone: (537) 645-1861

Villa Bárbara
Italian
Calle 100 No. 15121 e/ 5ta y
Arday, La Fortuna. Boyeros
Phone: (537) 643-9840

Lacoste
Caribbean
Avenida 225 No. 22506 e/ 210 y
211. Fontanar. Boyeros
Phone: (535) 293-7205

Tanokura
International
Calle 403 e/ 180 y 184, Santiago
de las Vegas. Boyeros
Phone: (537) 683-2173

Rancho Blanco
International
Calle 190 e/17 y 19 Reparto
Tessie, Santiago de las Vegas.
Phone: (537) 683-2992

La Flor de Loto (Lien Fa)
Chinese
Salud No. 313 e/ Gervasio y
Escobar. Centro Habana
Phone: (537) 860-8501

La Guarida
Caribbean
Concordia No. 418 e/ Gervasio y
Escobar. Centro Habana
Phone: (537) 866-9047

San Cristóbal
International
Calle San Rafael No.469 e/
Lealtad y Campanario. Centro
Habana
Phone: (537) 867-9109

Mimosa
Italian
Calle Salud No.317 e Gervasio y
Escobar. Centro Habana
Phone: (537) 867-1790

La California
International
Calle Crespo No. 5 e/ San Lázaro
y Refugio. Centro Habana
Phone: (537) 863-7510

Castropol
International
Calle Malecón No. 107 e/ Genio
Crespo. Centro Habana
Phone: (537) 861-4864

Bellomar
International
Virtudes 169 A e/ Industria y
Amistad. Centro Habana
Phone: (537) 861-0023

Versalles
International
San Lázaro No.14 e/ Cárcel y
Prado. Centro Habana
Phone: (537) 864-1339

El Cantonés
International
Manrique No. 564 altos e
Dragones y Salud. Centro
Habana
Phone: (537) 863-2981

El Levant
International
Águila e/ Reina y Dragones.
Centro Habana
Phone: (535) 805-0696

Min Chih Tang
Chinese
Manrique No. 513 (bajos) e/
Zanja y Dragones. Centro
Habana
Phone: (537) 863-2966

Wong Kong Ja Kong
Chinese
Dragones No. 414 esq.
Campanario. Centro Habana
Phone: (537) 863-2068

El Zarzal
International
Concordia No. 360 altos e/
Lealtad y Escobar.
Phone: (537) 862-5952

Notre Dame des Bijoux
International
Gervasio No. 218 e/ Concordia y
Virtudes. Centro Habana
Phone: (537) 860-6764

See Man
Chinese
Zanja No. 306 e/ Lealtad y
Escobar. Centro Habana
Phone: (537) 878-6484

PRIVATE RESTAURANTS
(HAVANA CITY)

Viejo Amigo
Chinese
Dragones 356 e/ San Nicolás y
Manrique. Centro Habana
Phone: (537) 861-8095

Mango Habana
International
Calle Industria No. 352 entre San
Miguel y San Rafael. Centro
Habana
Phone: (537) 861-4325

La Gitana
International
San Lázaro No.208 entre Águila
y Blanco. Centro Habana
Phone: (537) 866-6800

Torresson
Vegetarian
Malecón No. 27 e/ Prado y
Cárcel. Centro Habana
Phone: (537) 861-7476

Jared
International
Zanja No.165 e/ Manrique y San
Nicolás. Centro Habana
Phone: (537) 867-2063

El Maguey
International
Amistad No.111 e/ Ánimas y
Virtudes. Centro Habana
Phone: (537) 861-1701

Casa Miglis
Scandinavian
Lealtad No. 120 e/ Ánimas y
Laguna. Centro Habana
Phone: (537) 864-1486

Las Delicias de Consulado
International
Consulado No. 309 apto. B
e/Neptuno y Virtudes. Centro
Habana
Phone: (537) 863-7722

Chang Weng Chung Tong
Chinese
San Nicolás No. 517 e/ Zanja y
Dragones. Barrio Chino. Centro
Habana
Phone: (537) 862-1490

La Cayetana
International
Calle 20 de Mayo No. 529 e/
Marta Abreu y Línea del
Ferrocarril. Cerro
Phone: (537) 878-1991

Rancho Verde
International
Santa Catalina #10633 e/ Avenid
de los Ocujes y Palatino. Cerro
Phone: (537) 641-6433

El Taller
International
Calle 107 No. 2811 e/ 28 y 30.
Cotorro
Phone: (537) 682-2778

La Taberna
International
Avenida 101 No. 3006 e/ 30 y 32.
Cotorro
Phone: (537) 682-4608

El Resplandor
Caribbean
Calle 95 No. 3808 e/ 38 y 40.
Phone: (535) 276-8369

Rancho Coquito
French
San Miguel No. 566 e/ Anita y
Finlay, Víbora. Diez de Octubre
Phone: (537) 641-4463

La Orquídea
Caribbean
Lagueruela No.252 e/ 5ta y 6ta,
Lawton. Diez de Octubre
Phone: (537) 698-8210

Villa Hernández
Caribbean
Calle San Miguel, No. 112 e/
Revolución y Gelabert, Sevillano.
Diez de Octubre
Phone: (537) 640-5250

Melesio Grill
Grill
Calle Juan Delgado No. 676 e/
Freyre Andrade y Aranguren,
Sevillano. Diez de Octubre
Phone: (537) 642-4496

Snack Bar Mr. Montejo
Sandwiches
Calzada de 10 de Octubre e/
Vista Alegre y San Mariano.
Lawton. Diez de Octubre
Phone: (537) 641-5396

El Pavo
International
Vía Blanca No. 11 A e/ San Luis
y D. Guanabacoa
Phone: (537) 797-6432

117

PRIVATE RESTAURANTS
(HAVANA CITY)

U F C
International
Calle 3ra e/ 10 y 11. Reparto
Chivás. Guanabacoa
Phone: (537) 793-5919

Mangle Rojo
International
Avenida 1ra No. 2 e/ 11 y 12.
reparto Chivás. Guanabacoa
Phone: (537) 797-8613

Beti-Jai
Italian
Calle 11 No. 19 e/ 1ra y 3ra. Rptc
Chivás. Guanabacoa
Phone: (537) 793-5579

La Terracita
International
Villanueva No. 9606 e/ Concha y
Pezuela, Cojímar. Habana del
Este
Phone: (537) 766-6381

Chicken Little
International
Calle 504 No. 5B15 e/ 5taB y
5taC, Guanabo. Habana del Este
Phone: (537) 796-2351

Bodega Las Brisas
Seafood
Calle Real, No. 132 esq. Rio,
Cojimar. Habana del Este
Phone: (537) 766-7538

Don Peppo
Italian
482 #503 e/ 5taA y 5taD,
Guanabo. Habana del Este
Phone: (537) 796-4229

La Reina del Mar
International
Calle Real No. 110 e/ Chacón y
Focsa, Cojimar.. Habana del Este
Phone: (537) 766-7288

Califa
International
Calle Real,No. 31 esq. Moret,
Cojimar.. Habana del Este
Phone: (537) 766-7668

La Terraza de Cojimar
Seafood
Calle Real No. 161 esq
Candelaria, Cojimar.. Habana
del Este
Phone: (537) 766-5150

Italnova
Italian
5ta Avenida No. 48018 e/ 480 y
482. Guanabo. Habana del Este
Phone: (537) 796-7896

Luca's Bar & Grill
International
Calle 15 e/ 2da y 4ta. Reparto
Guiteras. Habana del Este
Phone: (537) 767-4279

Bellavista
International
482 #506 e/ 5taA y 5taD,
Guanabo. Habana del Este
Phone: (537) 796-3064

Ajiaco Café
Caribbean
Calle Los Pinos No. 267 e/ 3raE y
5ta. Cojímar. Habana del Este
Phone: (537) 765-0514

Piccolo
Italian
Ave 5ta e/ 502 y 504 Guanabo.
Habana del Este
Phone: (537) 796-4300

La Indiana
International
Calle 222 A No. 2302 e/ 23 y 23
A, La Coronela. La Lisa
Phone: (537) 272-7624

Don Francisco
International
Ave. 35 No. 11 411 e/ 114 y 116.
Marianao
Phone: (537) 262-0514

La Paila
Italian
Calle 88-B esq. a 51-A. Marianao
Phone: (537) 267-0282

Samaria
Caribbean
Calle 128 No. 6116 e/ 61 y 63.
Marianao
Phone: (537) 265-3393

Okan Tomi
International
114 No. 7117 e/ 71 y 73.
Marianao
Phone: (537) 260-6107

4 Palmas
International
Calle 1ra No. 38 e/ Vía Blanca y
Rotaria. Regla
Phone: (537) 794-2236

PRIVATE RESTAURANTS
(HAVANA CITY)

Dulcería Bianchini II
Pastry-confectionery
San Ignacio No. 68 Plaza de la
Catedral. Habana Vieja
Phone: (537) 862-8477

Doña Eutimia
Caribbean
Callejón del Chorro No.60 C,
Plaza de la Catedral. Habana
Vieja
Phone: (537) 861-1332

Habana 61
International
Habana No.61 e/ Cuarteles y
Peña Pobre. Habana Vieja
Phone: (537) 861-9433

Bar Restaurante Art Pub
International
Teniente Rey No. 306 e/
Aguacate y Compostela .
Habana Vieja
Phone: (537) 861-5014

Los Nardos
Spanish
Paseo del Prado No. 563 e/
Dragones y Teniente Rey. Phone
(537) 863-2985

Iván Chef Justo
International
Aguacate No.9 esquina a
Chacón. Habana Vieja
Phone: (537) 863-9697

El Asturianito
Italian
Paseo del Prado No. 563 e/
Dragones y Teniente Rey.
Phone: (537) 863-2985

El Tablao de Pancho
Italian
Zulueta No. 658 e/ Gloria y
Apodaca. Habana Vieja
Phone: (537) 861-7761

Mama Inés
International
Obrapía No.60 e/ Oficios y
Baratillo. Habana Vieja
Phone: (537) 862-2669

La Xana
Italian
Prado No. 309 esq. Virtudes.
Habana Vieja
Phone: (537) 864-1447

El Viejo Enrike
International
Calle Corrales No.161 e/ Aponte
y Cienfuegos. Habana Vieja
Phone: (537) 861-2989

Castillo de Farnés
Spanish
Monserrate, esquina a Obrapía.
Habana Vieja
Phone: (537) 867-1030

La Terraza
Brasserie
Prado No. 309 esq. Virtudes.
Habana Vieja
Phone: (537) 864-1447

**Café Boutique Jaqueline
Fumero**
French
Compostela No. 1 esq. Cuarteles
Habana Vieja
Phone: (537) 862-6562

El Fígaro
Caribbean
Aguiar No.18 e/ Peña Pobre y
Avenida de las Misiones.
Phone: (537) 861-0544

Casa Vieja
International
Habana No.203 esq. Tejadillo.
Habana Vieja
Phone: (537) 863-2927

El Mariachi
International
Obrapía No.454 e/ Aguacate y
Villegas. Habana Vieja
Phone: (537) 862-7677

Boaz
International
Inquisidor, No. 508 e/ Luz y
Acosta. Habana Vieja
Phone: (537) 862-3821

**La Moneda Cubana
(Empedrado)**
International
Empedrado No. 152 esq.
Mercader. Habana Vieja
Phone: (537) 861-5304

**La Moneda Cubana
(San Ignacio)**
San Ignacio No.77 e/ O'Reilly y
Empedrado. Habana Vieja
Phone: (537) 867-3852

Doña Blanquita
Caribbean
Prado No.158 e/ Colón y
Refugio, 1er piso. Habana Vieja
Phone: (537) 867-4958

PRIVATE RESTAURANTS
(HAVANA CITY)

La Julia
Caribbean
O'Reilly No.506 A e/ Bernaza y
Villegas. Habana Vieja
Phone: (537) 862-7438

La Taberna del Pescador
Seafood
Calle San Ignacio, No. 260 e/
Amargura y Lamparilla.
Phone: (537) 867-1629

Todo en TV
Caribbean
Egido entre Merced y Jesus
Maria. Habana Vieja
Phone: (537) 866-1911

Sevillas
Caribbean
Obispo No. 455 e/ Villegas y
Aguacate, 1er Piso, apto 2.
Habana Vieja
Phone: (537) 861-3705

Don Pucho
International
Aguacate No. 262 e/ Obispo y
Obrapía. Habana Vieja
Phone: (537) 862-3667

La Dueña
Caribbean
San Isidro No. 61 e/ Cuba y
Damas. Habana Vieja
Phone: (537) 860-0445

Chez Aimée
International
Compostela No. 157 e/ San Juan
de Dios y Empedrado.
Phone: (537) 863-3803

La Criolla
Caribbean
Calle San Ignacio No.68 e/
O'Reilly y Empedrado. Habana
Vieja
Phone: (537) 860-2210

Taberna El Portón
International
Merced No. 68C e/ San Ignacio y
Cuba. Habana Vieja
Phone: (537) 860-2592

La Deliciosa de la Habana
International
Bernaza No.1 apto. 1 1er piso e/
Obispo y O'Reilly . Habana Vieja
Phone: (537) 862-1534

Cuba Italia
Italian
Calle Cuba No. 215 e/
Empedrado y O'Reilly. Habana
Vieja
Phone: (537) 860-2266

La Perla de Obispo
International
Obispo No. 307 apto 1 e/ Habana
y Aguiar. Habana Vieja
Phone: (537) 861-6276

Pizzanella/Habana Vieja
Italian
Aguiar No.18 e/ Peña Pobre y
Avenida de las Misiones.
Phone: (537) 864-6527

El Cubano
International
Muralla No. 309 e/ Habana y
Compostela. Habana Vieja
Phone: (537) 863-0974

Las Estaciones
International
Amargura No. 254 e/ Habana y
Compostela.. Habana Vieja
Phone: (537) 864-8795

La Doña
International
Obispo No. 512 altos, e/ Bernaza
y Villegas.. Habana Vieja
Phone: (537) 866-2240

El Coco
International
Obispo No. 312 e/ Habana y
Aguiar. Habana Vieja
Phone: (537) 867-2107

La Gallega
International
Compostela e/ Obispo y O'Reilly
No. 255. Habana Vieja
Phone: (537) 867-3981

Rincón de Pancho
International
San Ignacio No. 68 e/ O'Reilly y
Empedrado, Apto 12.. Habana
Vieja
Phone: (537) 818-5325

Rancho Luna
International
San Ignacio, No. 68 e/ O'Reilly y
Empedrado apto 2.. Habana
Vieja
Phone: (537) 860-2221

Gonella
International
San Ignacio 68 e/ O'Reilly y
Empedrado, apto. 9.
Phone: (537) 867-1686

PRIVATE RESTAURANTS
(HAVANA CITY)

NaO
Caribbean
Obispo No. 1 e/ San Pedro (Ave. del Puerto) y Baratillo. Habana Vieja
Phone: (537) 295-8209

Don Lorenzo
Italian
Calle Acosta, No. 260 A e/ Habana y Compostela. Habana Vieja
Phone: (537) 861-6733

Bistró Habana Kohly (BHK)
International
Ave. 45 #2805 e/ 28 y 34. Playa
Phone: (537) 205-2616

Chino Lam
Chinese
Calle 3ra A e/ 84 y 86 #8410 Miramar. Playa
Phone: (537) 205-4052

La Proa
Grill
Calle 60 e/ 3ra y 3ra A. No.303 Miramar. Playa
Phone: (537) 205-1039

Rejoneo
International
11 esq.84 No.8220, Miramar. Playa
Phone: (537) 203-5190

Tic-Tac Boquitas
Snack food
11 esq.84 No.8220, Miramar
Phone: (537) 203-5190

Kpricho
International
3ra y 94. Playa
Phone: (537) 206-4167

Cubata Havana
Mexican
Calle 31 No. 3012 e/ 30 y 34. Playa
Phone: (537) 206-2540

Café Lavastida
International
Calle 1era e/ 42 y 44 No. 4215. Playa
Phone: (537) 202-7938

Rio Mar
International
3ra y Final #11, La Puntilla, Miramar. Playa
Phone: (537) 209-4838

El Palio
Snack food
Calle 1ra No. 2402 e/ 24 y 26, Miramar. Playa
Phone: (537) 202-9867

La Cocina de Lilliam
International
Calle 48 No. 1311 e/ 13 y 15. Playa
Phone: (537) 209-6514

Melen Club
International
Calle 1ra e/ 46 y 60, Miramar. Playa
Phone: (537) 203-0433

El Olivo
Spanish
Calle 36 No.303 e/ 3ra y 5ta. Miramar. Playa
Phone: (537) 203-7445

Espacios
International
Address: Calle 10 No.513 e/ 5ta y 7ma. Playa
Phone: (537) 202-2921

BellaHabana
International
Calle 6 No. 512 e/ 5b (calle 31) y 7ma, Miramar. Playa
Phone: (537) 203-8364

Tabarish
Russian
Calle 20 No. 503 e/ y 5ta y 7ma, Miramar. Playa
Phone: (537) 202-9188

Hecho en Casa
International
Calle 30 No. 106 e/ 1ra y 3ra, Miramar. Playa
Phone: (537) 203-6151

Élite
International
Calle 38 e/ 42 y 7ma No. 705. Playa
Phone: (537) 209-3260

La Buena Vida
Vegetarian
Calle 46 No. 917 e/ 9 y 11. Playa
Phone: (537) 202-5816

PRIVATE RESTAURANTS
(HAVANA CITY)

La Esperanza
International
Calle 16 No. 105 e/ 1ra y 3ra,
Miramar.. Playa
Phone: (537) 202-4361

El Diluvio
Italian
Calle 72 No. 1705 e/ 17 y 19.
Phone: (537) 202-1531

La Carboncita
Italian
3ra No. 3804 e/ 38 y 40. Playa
Phone: (535) 290-4984

Vistamar
International
Ave 1ra e/ 22 y 24, Miramar.
Phone: (537) 203-8328

Café Fortuna
Snack food
3ra entre 28 y 26, Miramar. Playa
Phone: (537) 203-3376

El Partenón
International
Calle 50 #1109 e/ 11 y 13. Playa
Phone: (537) 209-0405

Casa René
Italian
Calle 22 No. 3110 e/ 33 31 A
Miramar. Playa
Phone: (537) 205-3214

Milano Lounge Club
Italian
Calle 3ra No.2404 e/ 24 y 26
Miramar . Playa
Phone: (537) 203-4641

Doctor Café
International
28 No. 111 e/ 1ra y 3ra. Playa
Phone: (537) 203-4718

Chef Gusteau's
French
Calle 7ma A #6609 e/ 66 y 70.
Playa
Phone: (537) 203-4507

Casa Blanca/Taller de Sueños
International
Ave. 49 No. 3401 esq. a 34.
Reparto Kohly. Playa
Phone: (537) 203-7232

Cascada
International
Calle cero entre 1ra y 3ra,
Miramar. Playa
Phone: (537) 205-4999

Din Don
Italian
Calle 11 No. 7816 e/ 78 y 80..
Playa
Phone: (537) 203-0445

Segundo Piso
International
1ra No. 4407, e/ 44 y 46, apto 3.
Playa
Phone: (537) 205-9241

Cafesong
International
Calle 13 No. 7007 e/ 70 y 72.
Playa
Phone: (537) 209-3625

Cubanitos en 3B
International
Calle 9na No. 12018 esq. 130..
Playa
Phone: (535) 291-6983

Los Compadres
Mexican
Calle 66 A esq 41. Playa
Phone: (537) 203-6908

Mi Jardín
Mexican
Calle 66 no. 517 entre 5ta B y
7ma, Miramar. Playa
Phone: (537) 203-4627

Másquenada
Italian.
164 No.112 e/1ra y 5ta. Flores.
Playa
Phone: (535) 358-3198

Pizzería 22
Italian
Calle 22 No. 3306 A e/ 33 y 35,
Miramar. Playa
Phone: (537) 205-9341

Bom Apetíte
International
Calle 11 No.7210 e/ 72 y 74,
Miramar. Playa
Phone: (537) 203-3634

Mamy's
International
Calle 16 No.708 e/ 7ma y 31.
Playa
Phone: (537) 203-6700

PRIVATE RESTAURANTS
(HAVANA CITY)

Parrillada 84 y Quince
International
Ave. 84 esq. a 15 #8402. Playa
Phone: (537) 206-3430

Ranchón La Mulata
Caribbean
Calle 3ra A No. 9012 e/ 90 y 92.
Playa
Phone: (537) 203-8384

Real Café
International
Calle 7ma e/ 62 y 66. Playa
Phone: (537) 203-7219

Monte Barreto
International
Calle 9na, No. 7813, e/ 78 y 80,
Miramar. Playa
Phone: (537) 206-3527

Complejo Lucecita
Caribbean
Calle 182 esq. 15, Siboney. Playa
Phone: (537) 272-4673

Mulanché
Caribbean
Calle 19 No. 3602 esq. 36. Playa
Phone: (537) 202-9926

Chaplin's Café
Caribbean
Calle 8 No. 513 /5ta y 5ta B,
Miramar. Playa
Phone: (537) 202-1795

Las Marías
International
Calle 48 No. 1107 e/ 11 y 13.
Playa
Phone: (537) 209-2140

Vigía
Italian
Avenida 5ta No. 25804 e/ 258 y
260. Santa Fé. Playa
Phone: (537) 272-8183

La Fontana Habana
Caribbean
Calle 3raA esq. 46. Miramar.
Playa
Phone: (537) 202 8337

La Onda de David
International
Avenida 19 No. 7605 e/ 76 y 78.
Playa. Playa
Phone: (537) 209-5853

Casa Zule
Mediterranean
Calle 30 No 116 e/ 1ra y 3ra.
Miramar. Playa
Phone: (537) 202-3275

El Faro
Snack food
Calle 72 A #4106 e/ 41 A y 41 B.
Playa
Phone: (535) 284-4070

Pizzanella/Playa
Italian
Calle 33 No.4208 e/ 42 y 44. Play
Phone: (537) 203-2625

Barlovento
Mediterranean
Avenida 9na No. 12018 e 120 y
130, Reparto Cubanacán. Playa
Phone: (537) 208-2437

Voilá
International
14 No. 511 e/ 5ta y 7ma.
Miramar. Playa
Phone: (537) 202-5392

Calle Diez
International
Calle 10 No. 314 e/ 3ra y 5ta,
Miramar. Playa
Phone: (537) 209-6702

La Figura
International
Calle 64 esq. 45 No. 4316. Playa
Phone: (537) 203-0681

Dulce Habana
Italian
Calle 17 e/ D y E No. 511
Vedado. Plaza de la Revolución
Phone: (537) 830-4185

Bikos
Mediterranean
Calle 19 No.1010 e/ 10 y 12. Plaza
de la Revolución
Phone: (537) 831-8847

Razones
International
Calle F No. 63 apto 2 e/ 3ra y 5ta,
Vedado. Plaza de la Revolución
Phone: (537) 830-6055

El Acertijo
International
Calle 27 No. 510 e/ E y F.,
Vedado.. Plaza de la Revolución
Phone: (537) 831-1744

PRIVATE RESTAURANTS
(HAVANA CITY)

El Litoral
Seafood
Malecón 161 e/ K y L.
Plaza de la Revolución
Phone: (537) 830-2201

Motivos
International
Calle F No. 63 e/ 3ra y 5ta
Vedado. Plaza de la Revolución
Phone: (537) 832-8732

El Cocinero
International
Calle 26 S/N e/ 11 y 13, Vedado.
Plaza de la Revolución
Phone: (537) 832-2355

Abdala
Grill
Calle D e/ 15 y 17. Vedado. Plaza
de la Revolución
Phone: (535) 832-1443

Starbien
International
Calle 29 No.205 e/ B y C.
Vedado. Plaza de la Revolución
Phone: (537) 830-0711

Las Tierras del Sol
Italian
Calle 23 esq 8 No. 1604, Vedado.
Plaza de la Revolución
Phone: (535) 298-3379

La Catedral
International
Calle 8 e/ Calzada y 5ta, Vedado
Plaza de la Revolución
Phone: (537) 830-0793

Madrigal
International
Calle 17 No. 809 (altos), e/ 2 y 4,
Vedado. Plaza de la Revolución
Phone: (537) 831-2433

El Jardín de los Milagros
Caribbean
Calle 37 No. 817 e/ 24 y San Juan
Bautista. Nuevo Vedado.
Phone: (537) 881-1053

Café Presidente
Italian
Calle 25 esq G, Vedado. Plaza de
la Revolución
Phone: (537) 832-3091

Bar Encuentros
Mediterranean
Línea #112 e/L y M. Plaza de la
Revolución
Phone: (537) 832-9744

Café-Galería Mamainé
Caribbean
Calle L No. 206 e/ 15 y 17,
Vedado. Plaza de la Revolución
Phone: (537) 832-8328

Bar Restaurante
Mediterráneo Havana
Mediterranean
Calle 13 No. 406 e/ F y G. Plaza
de la Revolución
Phone: (537) 832-4894

Piso 15
Japaneese
Calle 15 No. 152, piso 15 apto
142 e/ L y K, Vedado.
Phone: (537) 832-4945

Al frío y al fuego
Snack food
Calle 25 No. 672 e/ E y F,
Vedado. Plaza de la Revolución
Phone: (537) 831-8243

Bar Bohemio
International
Calle 21 No 1065 entre 12 y 14.
Plaza de la Revolución
Phone: (537) 833-6918

Atelier
International
Calle 5ta No. 511 e/ Paseo y 2.
Vedado. Plaza de la Revolución
Phone: (537) 836-2025

Porto-Habana
International
Calle E No.158 B e/Calzada y
9na Piso 11. Plaza de la
Revolución
Phone: (537) 833-1425

Piano Bar Restaurante
Somavilla
International
Calle 15 No. 313 esq. H, Vedado.
Plaza de la Revolución
Phone: (537) 832-7323

El Recanto
International
Calle 10, No.401 esq 17, Vedado.
Plaza de la Revolución
Phone: (537) 830-4396

El Beduino
International
5ta No.607 e/ 4 y 6. Vedado.
Plaza de la Revolución
Phone: (535) 295-2093

PRIVATE RESTAURANTS
(HAVANA CITY)

Café Laurent
International
Calle M No. 257 e/19 y 21.
Vedado. Plaza de la Revolución
Phone: (537) 832-6890

Brasilerísimo
Brasileña
Calle 3ra No. 261 e/ A y B,
Vedado. Plaza de la Revolución
Phone: (537) 831-6329

PP's Teppanyaki
Japaneese
Calle 21 No 106 e/ L y M.
Vedado. Plaza de la Revolución
Phone: (537) 836-2530

Mesón Sancho Panza
International
Calle J e/ 23 y 25. Plaza de la
Revolución
Phone: (537) 831-2862

La Casona de 21
International
Calle 21 No. 857 e/ 4 y 6, Vedadc
Plaza de la Revolución
Phone: (537) 831-6063

La Onza
Spanish
21 esq B No 615, Vedado. Plaza
de la Revolución
Phone: (537) 830-2939

El Balcón
International
Calle 28 No. 590, e/ 31 y 33,
Nuevo Vedado. Plaza de la
Revolución
Phone: (537) 831-2959

Casa Lala
International
Calle 24 e/ 23 y 21. Plaza de la
Revolución
Phone: (537) 830-1410

Decamerón
International
Línea No.753 e/ Paseo y 2,
Vedado. Plaza de la Revolución
Phone: (537) 832-2444

Juana la Cubana
International
Calle 19 No. 1101 esq. a 14.
Vedado. Plaza de la Revolución
Phone: (537) 831-9968

Bollywood Havana
Hindi
Calle 35 No.1361 e/ 26 y 24,
Nuevo Vedado. Plaza de la
Revolución
Phone: (537) 883-1216

La Chuchería
Snack food
Calle 1ra e/ C y D, Vedado. Plaz
de la Revolución
Phone: (537) 830-0708

El Idilio
Grill
Avenida de los Presidentes No.
351, esq. 15. Vedado. Plaza de la
Revolución
Phone: (537) 832-8182

Café Light
International
Calle Línea No. 58 e/ M y N,
Vedado. Plaza de la Revolución
Phone: (537) 831-6351

23 y 6
Italian
Calle 23 No. 1011 e/ 4 y 6,
Vedado. Plaza de la Revolución
Phone: (537) 835-3293

El Farallón
International
Calle 22 No. 361, esq. 23,
Vedado. Plaza de la Revolución
Phone: (537) 830-5187

Q'Rico
Italian
Calle 23 No.1106 e/ 8 y 10,
Vedado. Plaza de la Revolución
Phone: (537) 833-9435

La Pachanga
Snack food
Calle 28 No. 254 / 21 y 23,
Vedado. Plaza de la Revolución
Phone: (537) 830-2507

El Quijote
International
23 No.402 e/ I y J, Vedado. Plaza
de la Revolución
Phone: (537) 832-6313

Snack Bar 911
Snack food
Calle 27 e/ 4 y 6 # 901. Plaza de la
Revolución
Phone: (537) 833-1783

El Pachanguero
International
San Lázaro 1217 entre Mazón y
Basarrate. Plaza de la Revolución
Phone: (537) 879-9527

PRIVATE RESTAURANTS
(HAVANA CITY)

Black & White
International
Calle 12 No. 508 e/ 21 y 23 apto 1
Plaza de la Revolución
Phone: (537) 836-9301

La Casa
Japaneese
Calle 30 No. 865 e/ Avenida 26 y
41.Nuevo Vedado. Plaza de la
Revolución
Phone: (537) 881-7000

Esencia Habana
International
Calle B No. 153 e/ Calzada y
Línea. Plaza de la Revolución
Phone: (537) 836-3031

Gringo Viejo
International
Calle 21 No. 454 e/ E y F.
Vedado. Plaza de la Revolución
Phone: (537) 831-1946

Don Remigio
International
Calle 36 No. 96 e/41 y 43, Nuevo
Vedado. Plaza de la Revolución
Phone: (537) 881-8058

El Balcón del Edén
International
Calle K No. 361 e/ 19 y 21. Plaza
de la Revolución
Phone: (537) 832-9113

El Loco Loco
Snack food
Neptuno No. 1155 esq. Infanta.
Plaza de la Revolución
Phone: (537) 873-2548

Aries
International
Ave. Universidad No. 456 e/ J y
K, Vedado. Plaza de la
Revolución
Phone: (537) 832-4118

Mamma Mía
Italian
Calle 23 e/ 22 y 24, Vedado.
Plaza de la Revolución
Phone: (537) 831-3093

Toke
Snack food
Calle 25 esq Infanta. Plaza de la
Revolución
Phone: (537) 836-3440

Punto G
International
17 No. 360 esq. G. Vedado. Plaza
de la Revolución
Phone: (537) 832-8354

La Moraleja
International
Calle 25 No. 454 e/ J e I. Plaza de
la Revolución
Phone: (537) 832-0963

La Tarequera
International
Calle 24 No. 418 e/ 23 y 25,
Vedado. Plaza de la Revolución
Phone: (537) 836-3636

Habitania
International
Calle 30 No. 964 e/ 26 y 47.
Nuevo Vedado.
Phone: (537) 881-2026

Nerei
International
Calle 19 No 110 esquina a L.
Vedado. Plaza de la Revolución
Phone: (537) 832-7860

M en A
International
Calle 25 No. 158 e/ Infanta y O.
Plaza de la Revolución
Phone: (537) 836-7985

Donde Dorian
Snack food
25 #1616 e/ 26 y 28. Plaza de la
Revolución
Phone: (537) 831-1241

Le Chansonnier
International
Calle J No. 257 e/ 15 y Línea,
Vedado. Plaza de la Revolución
Phone: (537) 832-1576

Monguito
International
Calle L No. 408 e/ 23 y 25. Plaza
de la Revolución
Phone: (537) 831-2615

Santa Bárbara
International
Calle M e/ 17 y Línea No. 162.
Plaza de la Revolución
Phone: (537) 832-7251

La Antonia
International
Calle Mazón No. 4 e/ Neptuno y
San Miguel, Vedado .
Plaza de la Revolución
Phone: (537) 873-5286

INDEX

16833440R00074

Made in the USA
Middletown, DE
22 December 2014